UKULELE FRETBOARD ROADMAPS

THE ESSENTIAL PATTERNS THAT ALL THE PROS KNOW AND USE

BY FRED SOKOLOW & JIM BELOFF

Speed • Pitch • Balance • Loop

To access audio visit:
www.halleonard.com/mylibrary

Enter Code
4042-2204-1673-8428

The Recording

Fluke Ukulele, Other Stringed Instruments, and Vocals—Fred Sokolow
Sound Engineer and Other Instruments—Dennis O'Hanlon
Recorded at O'Hanlon Recording and Music Services

with editorial assistance by Ronny Schiff

ISBN 978-1-4234-0041-7

7777 W. BLUEMOUND RD. P.O. BOX 13819 MILWAUKEE, WI 53213

In Australia Contact:
Hal Leonard Australia Pty. Ltd.
4 Lentara Court
Cheltenham, Victoria, 3192 Australia
Email: ausadmin@halleonard.com

Visit Hal Leonard Online at
www.halleonard.com

CONTENTS

INTRODUCTION

Accomplished ukulele players can ad lib hot solos and play backup in any key—all over the fretboard. They know several different soloing approaches and can choose the style that fits the tune, whether it's Hawaiian, Tin Pan Alley, folk, Dixieland, country, blues, rock, or jazz.

There are moveable patterns on the uke fretboard that make it easy to do these things. The pros are aware of these "fretboard roadmaps," even if they don't read music. Whether you want to jam with other players or be an accomplished solo uke player, this is essential knowledge.

You need the fretboard roadmaps if...

- You don't know how to play in every key.

- Your uke fretboard beyond the 5th fret is uncharted territory.

- Certain chords are mysterious and unknown.

- You've memorized a few tunes on the uke, but you don't have a system that ties it all together.

- You can strum a tune to back up your singing, but you can't play an instrumental solo.

Read on, and many mysteries will be explained. If you're serious about playing the ukulele, the pages that follow can shed light and save you a great deal of time.

Good luck,

Fred Sokolow and Jim Beloff

THE RECORDING AND THE PRACTICE TRACKS
All the licks, riffs, and tunes in this book are played on the accompanying audio.

There are also four practice tracks on the recording. They are mixed so that the uke is on one side of your stereo and the backup band is on the other.

Each track illustrates one or more *Roadmap* concepts, such as bluesy soloing, or circle-of-fifths chord progressions. By adjusting the balance in Playback+, you can tune out the uke track and practice playing along with the backup tracks.

PRELIMINARIES

TUNING

This book teaches ukulele in the *C tuning* (also called *C6 tuning*) because it's by far the most widespread tuning currently in use. There's a section at the end on D6 tuning, baritone tuning, and other tunings as well.

Use audio track 1 or a tuning device to tune up so you can play along with the songs on the audio. If one string is correctly tuned to an outside source, you can use the string-to-string method described below to tune the others.

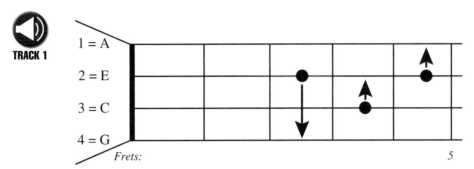

As the above diagram shows, once you've tuned the open 3rd (C) string, you can
- Tune the 2nd string (E) by matching it to the 3rd string/4th fret,
- Tune the 1st string (A) by matching it to the 2nd string/5th fret,
- Tune the 4th string (G) by matching it to the 2nd string/3rd fret.

A well-tuned ukulele will produce the "My Dog Has Fleas" melody or a C6 chord when you strum the strings from 4 to 1.

STRUMMING PATTERNS

Most people strum the ukulele with their fingers, while some use a felt pick. Either way, the movement comes from your wrist, not your arm.

Some use the thumb for downstrokes and index finger for upstrokes; others use the index finger for both up and downstrokes. Any variation that works for you is fine. If you choose to use a pick, hold it like this:

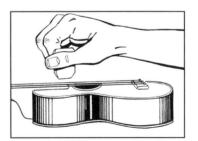

The strums on Tracks 2, 3, 4, and 5 are played on open unfretted strings (a C6 chord).

BASIC STRUM, 4/4 TIME

1. Strum down with the thumb, index finger, or pick.
2. Then strum up with the index finger or pick.
3. Repeat 1 and 2, three more times, to create this 4/4 rhythm:

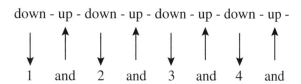

Listen to the track to hear how you can create a shuffle beat or a straight-eighths rock groove with this simple strum, just by changing your emphasis.

BASIC STRUM VARIATION 1

Here's one of many possible variations of the basic strum: leave out the first "and." In other words…

1. Strum down with the thumb, index finger, or pick.
2. Strum down again with thumb, index, or pick.
3. Strum up with index finger or pick.
4. Repeat steps 2 and 3, two more times.

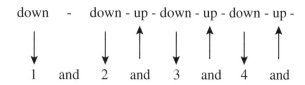

BASIC STRUM VARIATION 2

One more variation: use the previous strum and leave out the third downstroke.

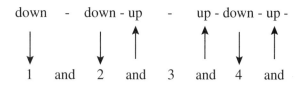

WALTZ STRUM, 3/4 TIME

Here's a 3/4 time strum:

1. Strum down with thumb, index finger, or pick.
2. Strum down with thumb, index finger, or pick.
3. Strum down with thumb, index finger, or pick.
4. Strum up with index finger or pick.

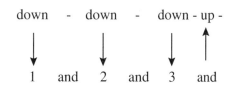

PICKING PATTERNS

Some players use banjo-type rolls on the uke. The thumb, index, and middle fingers execute rapid, three-finger rolls.

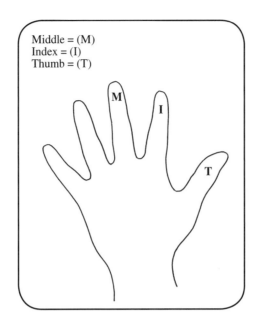

Here are some typical picking patterns:

TRACK 6

Forward Roll

I M T I M T I M

In-and-Out Roll

T I T M T I T M

Forward-Backward Roll

T I M T M I T M

FIRST POSITION CHORDS

Here are some basic chords. The numbers indicate fingering. Strum all four strings for each.

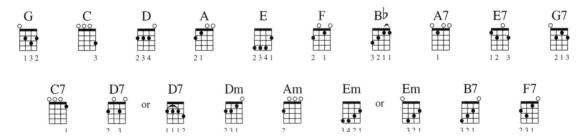

G   C   D   A   E   F   B♭   A7   E7   G7

C7   D7   D7   Dm   Am   Em   Em   B7   F7

STRUMMING SOME SIMPLE TUNES

The following tunes will give you a chance to practice chord changes and the above strums and picking patterns. Listen to each song before you start playing. Play each one as slowly as you need to in order to keep the rhythm smooth and steady. As soon as you can, play along with the recording.

SLOOP JOHN B.

Use the strum from Track 4, a variation of the 4/4 strum.

TRACK 7

C

We come on the Sloop John B., my grandfather and me.

G7

Around Nassau Town we did roam.

C   F

Drinking all night, got into a fight.

C   G7   C

I feel so broke up, I want to go home.

WHEN THE SAINTS GO MARCHING IN

Use the strum from Track 3, a variation of the basic 4/4 strum.

TRACK 8

G   D7

Oh, when the saints go marching in, oh, when the saints go marching in.

G   C   G   D7   G

Oh, Lord, I want to be in that number, when the saints go marching in.

AMAZING GRACE

Use the waltz strum from Track 5.

TRACK 9

D   G   D   A7

Amazing grace, how sweet the sound that saved a wretch like me.

D   D7   G   D   A7  D

I once was lost but now I'm found, was blind but now I see.

GAMBLER'S BLUES

Use the basic 4/4 strum from Track 2.

TRACK 10

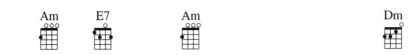

I was down in old Joe's barroom, at the corner of the square.

The drinks were served as usual, and the usual crowd was there.

ATTENTION GUITAR PLAYERS!

In case you haven't noticed, the ukulele is tuned like the top four (treble) strings of the guitar, but "up a 4th," or five frets higher. That means you can play all your guitar chords, at least four-string versions of them… and the names change up a 4th. Your guitar G chord is now a C, your D7 is now called G7, and so on. Of course that octave-higher 4th string will make things sound a bit different. But you've got quite a head start.

NOTES ON THE FRETBOARD

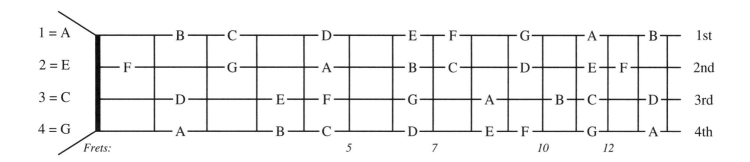

WHY? Knowing where the notes are will help you find chords and scales up and down the neck. It will help you alter and understand chords (e.g., *Why is this chord minor instead of major? How do I flat the seventh in this chord?*). It's a first step toward understanding music.

WHAT? **The notes get higher in pitch as you go up the alphabet and up the fretboard.**

A whole step is two frets, and a half step is one fret.

Sharps are one fret higher: 2nd string/1st fret = F, so 2nd string/2nd fret = F♯.

Flats are one fret lower: 3rd string/2nd fret = D, so 3rd string/1st fret = D♭.

HOW? **The uke is tuned G–C–E–A (from 4th to 1st string). Start by learning these notes!**

Fretboard markings help. Most ukuleles have fretboard inlays or marks on the neck indicating the 5th, 7th, 10th, and 12th frets. Become aware of these signposts.

DO IT! Learn other notes in reference to the notes you already know:

The notes at the 2nd fret of strings 1, 3, and 4 are a whole step (or one step of the alphabet) **higher than the open-string (unfretted) notes.** The 3rd string/open (unfretted) = C, so the 3rd string/2nd fret = D.

Everything starts over at the 12th fret. The open 1st string is A, so the 1st string/12th fret is also A.

You already know some notes from the string-to-string tuning method (from the Preliminaries section). The 3rd string/4th fret = E, the 2nd string/5th fret = A, and the 2nd string/3rd fret = G).

Learn the notes on the 1st string, and you'll also know the 4th string notes. The 4th string notes are just two frets higher.

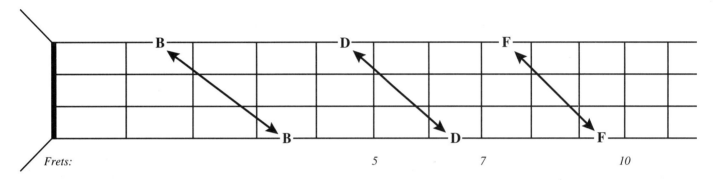

The 3rd string, three frets below the 1st string, is the same note an octave lower.

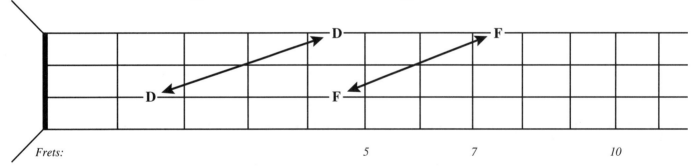

The 4th string, three frets below the 2nd string, is the same note.

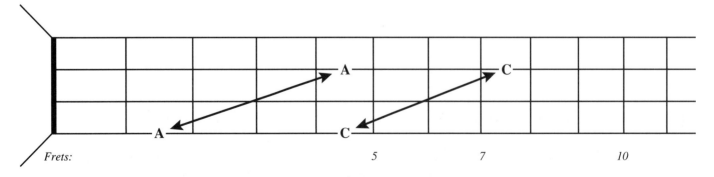

SUMMING UP—NOW YOU KNOW...

1. The location of the notes on the fretboard and some shortcuts to memorizing them.

2. The meanings of these musical terms:
   a) Whole Step
   b) Half Step
   c) Sharp (♯)
   d) Flat (♭)

THE MAJOR SCALE

C Major Scale

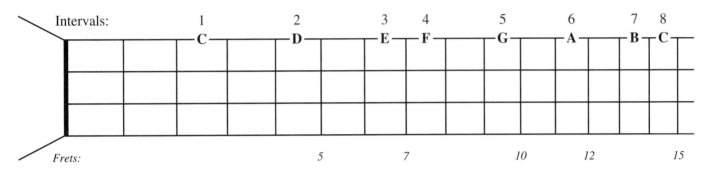

WHY? To understand music and to communicate with other players, you need to know about the major scale. The major scale is a ruler that helps you measure distances between notes and chords. Knowing the major scale will help you understand and talk about chord construction, scales, and chord relationships.

WHAT? **The major scale is the "Do-Re-Mi" scale you have heard all your life.** Countless familiar tunes are composed of notes from this scale.

Intervals **are distances between notes.** The intervals of the major scale are used to describe these distances. For example, E is the third note of the C major scale, and it is four frets above C (see above). This distance is called a *3rd*. Similarly, A is a 3rd above F, and C♯ is a 3rd above A. On the ukulele, a 3rd is always a distance of four frets.

HOW? **Every major scale has the same interval pattern of whole and half steps:**
In other words, the major scale ascends by whole steps (two frets at a time) with two excep-

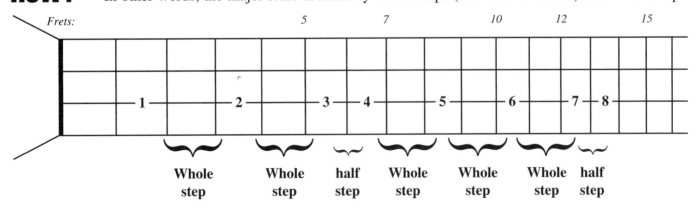

tions: there is a half step (one fret) from the third to the fourth notes and from the seventh to the eighth notes. It's helpful to think of intervals in terms of frets (e.g., a 3rd is four frets).

Intervals can extend above the octave. They correspond to lower intervals:

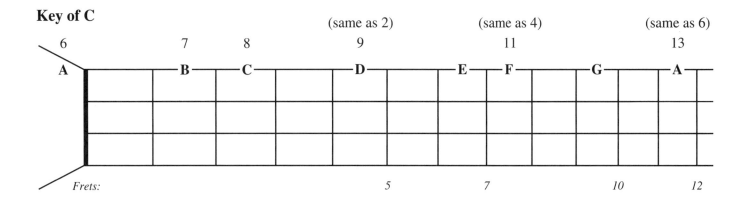

DO IT! **Learn the major scale intervals** by playing any note and finding the note that is a 3rd higher, a 4th, a 5th higher, etc.

SUMMING UP—NOW YOU KNOW...

The intervals of the major scale and the number of frets that make up each interval.

THE MOVEABLE D FORMATION AND ITS VARIATIONS

E Chords:

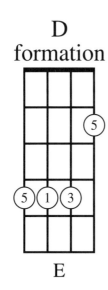

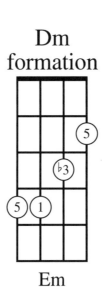

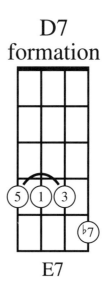

WHY? **ROADMAPS #3, 4,** and **5** will help you build a full chord vocabulary. These three chapters have all the chords you'll need to play any song. And if you read on, you'll understand how the chords are constructed, which makes learning them much easier.

WHAT? **A chord is a group of three or more notes played simultaneously.**

A moveable chord can be played all over the fretboard. It contains no open (unfretted) strings.

The root is the note that gives a chord its name.

There are three main types of chords: major, minor, and seventh chords. Each type has a distinct sound that you will come to recognize. Each chord type is made by combining specific notes.

   • **Major chords consist of a root, 3rd, and 5th.** For example, D major is made of the 1st, 3rd, and 5th notes of the D major scale: D–F♯–A.

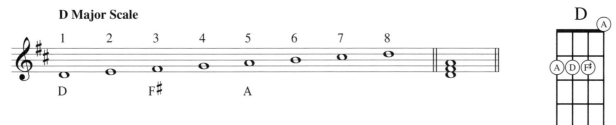

- **Minor chords consist of a root, ♭3rd, and 5th.** Dm = D–F–A.

- **7th chords consist of a root, 3rd, 5th, and ♭7th.** D7 = D–F♯–A–C.

In **ROADMAP #3** the intervals of the D, Dm, and D7 formations are indicated by the numerals.

The D formation is so named because it's a moveable version of the first position D chord. If you move the D chord up a fret, you have to fret the 1st string to bring it up a fret as well. That gives you a moveable chord:

D

D#

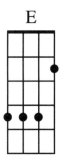
E

Wherever you play the D formation on the fretboard, it's always a major chord, and the 3rd string is always the root.

The three D formations of ROADMAP #3 are E chords, since they are "up two frets," where

their roots (the 3rd string at the 4th fret) are E notes.

HOW?

The 3rd string is the root of the D, Dm, and D7 formations. If you know the notes on the 3rd string, you can play these chord formations all over the fretboard and identify them by that string. In the diagrams below, the number to the right of the grid shows the fret number of your first (index) finger.

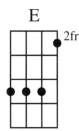
E   2fr

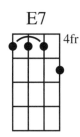
E7   4fr

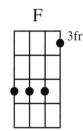
F   3fr

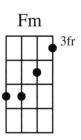
Fm   3fr

There are many ways to vary a major, minor, and seventh chord to make the chord more colorful without changing its basic identity. D major can be Dmaj7, D6, Dsus4, etc.

Many of these subtle chord variations resemble the basic major, minor, and 7th chord shapes—with one note added, or one note flatted or sharped.

DO IT!

Play the three moveable formations (D major formation, Dm formation, and D7 formation) all over the fretboard and name them.

Compare every new chord you learn to a basic chord you already know. Every small chord grid in the "DO IT" section below is a variation of a basic chord formation.

Here are the most-played chords. Play them and compare each formation to the larger grid to the left, from which it is derived. For consistency, all the forms are written as E chords.

D Major Formation (E chord)

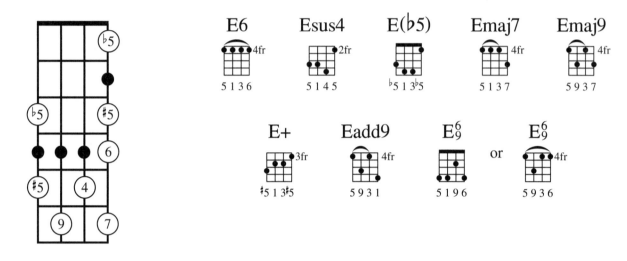

D Minor Formation (Em chord)

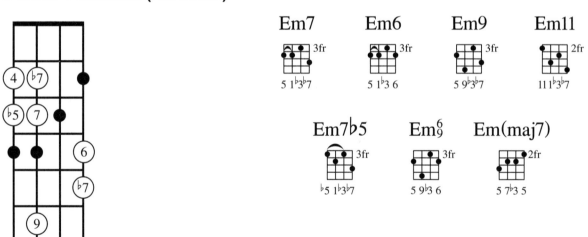

D7th Formation (E7 chord)

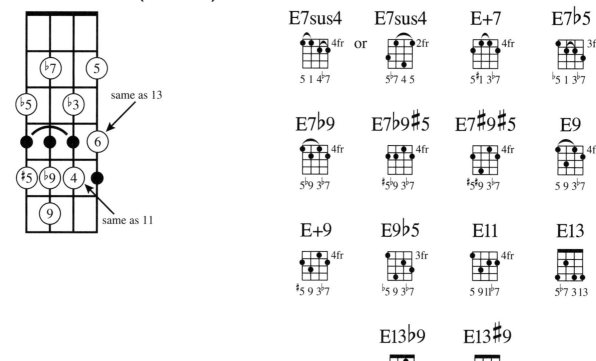

E7sus4 ... or ... **E7sus4** ... **E+7** ... **E7♭5**

5 1 4♭7 ... 5♭7 4 5 ... 5♯1 3♭7 ... ♭5 1 3♭7

E7♭9 ... **E7♭9♯5** ... **E7♯9♯5** ... **E9**

5♭9 3♭7 ... ♭5♭9 3♭7 ... ♯5♯9 3♭7 ... 5 9 3♭7

E+9 ... **E9♭5** ... **E11** ... **E13**

♯5 9 3♭7 ... ♭5 9 3♭7 ... 5 9 11♭7 ... 5♭7 3 13

E13♭9 ... **E13♯9**

5♭7♭9 13 ... 5♭7♯9 13

Diminished 7th

The diminished seventh chord formula is 1, ♭3, ♭5, ♭♭7. A diminished chord is like a 7th chord with everything flatted except the root. Diminished chords repeat every three frets. The following are all E diminished chords:

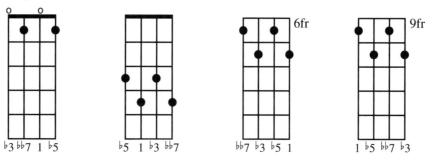

♭3 ♭♭7 1 ♭5 ... ♭5 1 ♭3 ♭♭7 ... ♭♭7 ♭3 ♭5 1 ... 1 ♭5 ♭♭7 ♭3

A diminished chord can be named by any of its four notes. For example, D° can also be called F°, A♭°, or B°, depending on the context in which it occurs.

SUMMING UP—NOW YOU KNOW...

1. Three moveable "D chord formations" (major, minor, and 7th) and how to play them all over the fretboard.

2. The formulas for major, minor, 7th, and diminished chords, and how to play them using moveable formations.

3. How to vary the moveable major, minor, and 7th chords to play dozens of chord types: minor 7ths, 6ths, major 7ths, etc.

4. The meanings of these musical terms:
   a) Chord
   b) Moveable Chord
   c) Root

THE MOVEABLE G FORMATION AND ITS VARIATIONS

A Chords:

G
formation

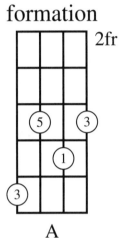

A

Gm
formation

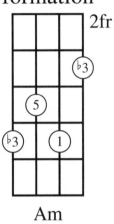

Am

G7
formation

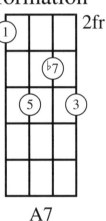

A7

WHY? The three G formations of **ROADMAP #4** will help you learn another entire set of moveable chords.

WHAT? **The G formation is so named because it's a moveable version of the first position G chord.** Wherever you play it on the fretboard, it's always a major chord, and the 2nd string is always the root.

A

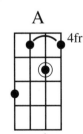

B♭

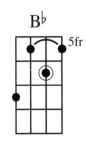

B

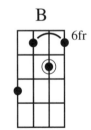

C

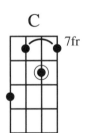

The three G formations of **ROADMAP #4** are A, Am, and A7 chords.

HOW?

The 2nd string is the root of the G and Gm formations. If you know the notes on the 2nd string, you can play these chord formations all over the fretboard and identify them by that string:

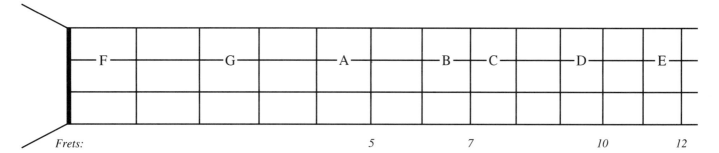

Frets: 5   7   10   12

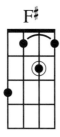 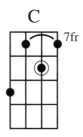 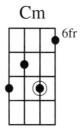 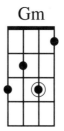

F#   C   Cm   Gm

The 4th string is the root of the G7 formation. If you know the notes on the 4th string, you can play G7 chord formations all over the fretboard and identify them by that string:

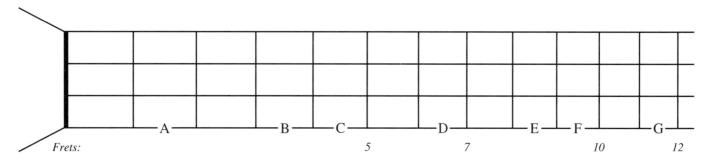

Frets: 5   7   10   12

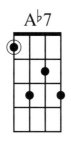 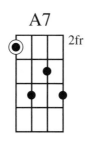 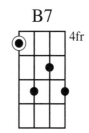 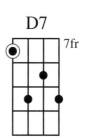

A♭7   A7   B7   D7

DO IT! Play the three moveable formations (G major formation, Gm formation, and G7 formation) all over the fretboard and name them.

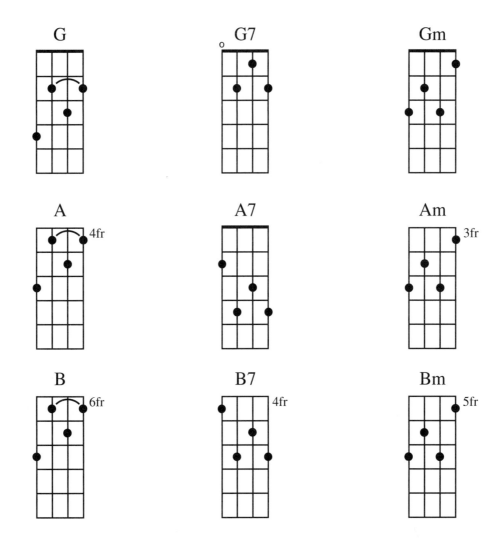

Compare every new chord you learn to a basic chord you already know. Every small chord grid in the "DO IT" section below is a variation of a basic chord formation.

Here are the most-played chords. Play them and compare each formation to the larger grid to the left, from which it is derived. For consistency's sake, they are all A chords.

G Major Formation (A Chord)

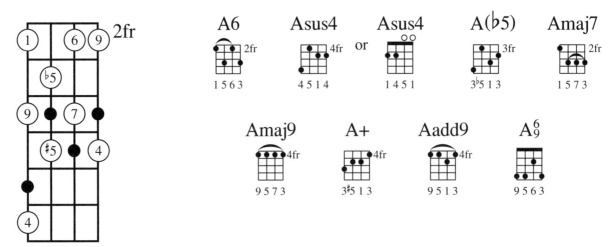

G Minor Formation (Am Chord)

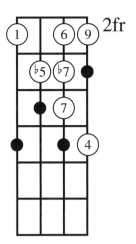

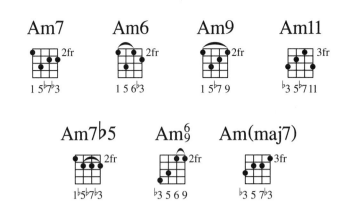

G7 Formation (A7 Chord)

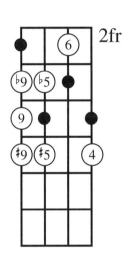

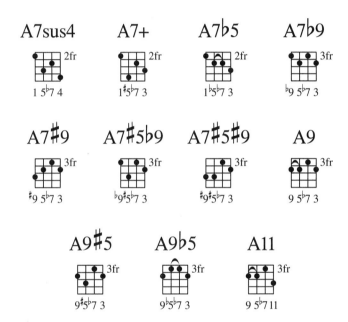

SUMMING UP—NOW YOU KNOW...

1. Three moveable G chord formations (major, minor, and 7th) and how to play them all over the fretboard.

2. How to vary the moveable major, minor, and 7th chords to play dozens of chord types: minor 7ths, 6ths, major 7ths, etc.

THE MOVEABLE B FORMATION AND ITS VARIATIONS

B Chords:

B
formation

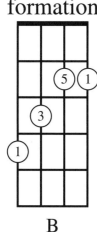

B

Bm
formation

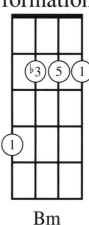

Bm

B7
formation

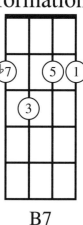

B7

WHY?   The three B formations of **ROADMAP #5** will help you learn another whole set of moveable chords.

WHAT?   **The B formation is so named because it's a moveable version of a second position B chord.** Wherever you play it on the fretboard, it's always a major chord, and the 1st and 4th strings are always the root.

B♭
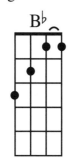

B
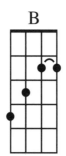

C
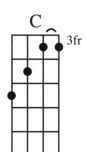
3fr

22

HOW?

The 1st and 4th strings are the roots of the B and Bm formations. The 1st string is the root of the B7 formation. If you know the notes on these strings, you can play the B chord formations all over the fretboard and identify them:

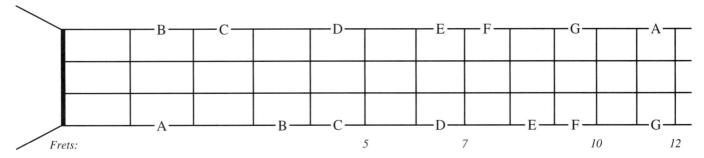

Frets:

DO IT!

Play the three moveable formations (B major formation, B7 formation, and Bm formation) all over the fretboard and name them in each position.

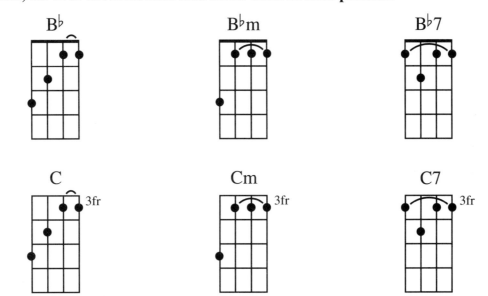

Compare every new chord you learn to a basic chord you already know. Every small chord grid in the "DO IT" section that follows is a variation of a basic chord formation.

Here are the most-played chords. Play them and compare each formation to the larger grid to the left, from which it is derived.

B Major Formation (B Chord)

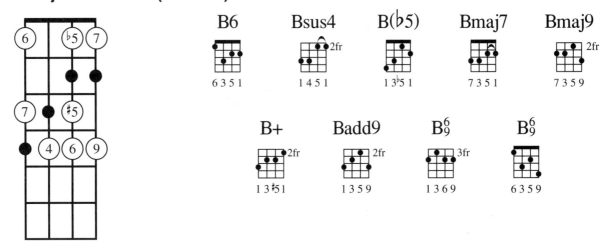

B Minor Formation (Bm Chord)

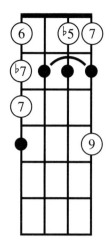

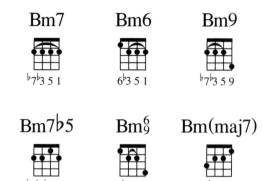

Bm7   Bm6   Bm9

♭7 3 5 1   6 ♭3 5 1   ♭7 ♭3 5 9

Bm7♭5   Bm⁶₉   Bm(maj7)

♭7 ♭3 ♭5 1   6 ♭3 5 9   7 ♭3 5 7

B7th Formation (B7 Chord)

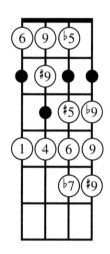

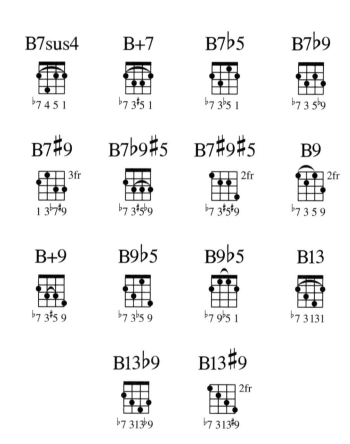

B7sus4   B+7   B7♭5   B7♭9

♭7 4 5 1   ♭7 3 ♯5 1   ♭7 3 ♭5 1   ♭7 3 5 ♭9

B7♯9   B7♭9♯5   B7♯9♯5   B9

1 3 ♭7 ♯9   ♭7 3 ♯5 ♭9   ♭7 3 ♯5 ♯9   ♭7 3 5 9

B+9   B9♭5   B9♭5   B13

♭7 3 ♯5 9   ♭7 3 ♭5 9   ♭7 9 ♭5 1   ♭7 3 13 1

B13♭9   B13♯9

♭7 3 13 ♭9   ♭7 3 13 ♯9

SUMMING UP—NOW YOU KNOW...

1. Three moveable "B chord formations" (major, minor, and 7th) and how to play them all over the fretboard.

2. How to vary the moveable major, minor, and 7th chords to play dozens of chord types: minor 7ths, 6ths, major 7ths, etc.

THE G–D–B ROADMAP

G Chords

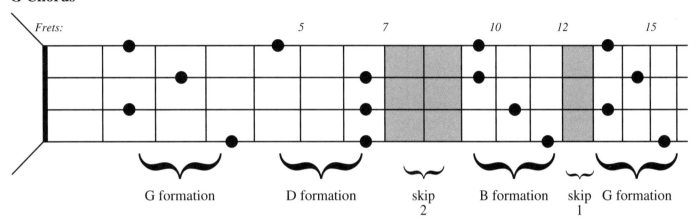

| G formation | D formation | skip 2 | B formation | skip 1 | G formation |

WHY? The G–D–B Roadmap shows you how to play any major chord all over the fretboard, using the three major chord formations of **ROADMAPS #3, 4,** and **5**. It's useful for locating chords up and down the neck and for finding a higher voicing of a chord.

WHAT? The chords in the fretboard diagram above are all G chords. Play them and see!

HOW? **To memorize this roadmap, remember: G, D–SKIP 2, B–SKIP 1.** In other words, to play G chords up and down the uke fretboard:

- Play a G formation at the 2nd fret (that's a G chord)…
- Then play a D formation starting at the next fret; that's the next G chord…
- Then skip two frets and play a B formation; that's the next G chord…
- Then skip one fret and play a G formation again; that's a still-higher G chord.

Okay, you probably can't play that last G formation/G chord; it's partly off the fretboard of most ukes. But it makes a major point about this roadmap:

The G–D–B Roadmap is an endless loop. It keeps repeating until you run out of frets.

You can start the G–D–B loop with any chord formation. It can start with the D formation and become the D–B–G loop. The fret spacing is the same no matter where you start. For example, here are all the E♭ chords, starting with the D formation E♭ chord:

E♭ Chords

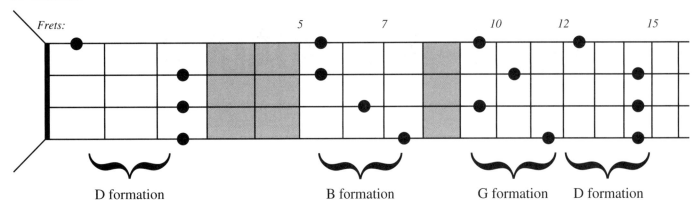

You can also start with the B formation. Here are all the C chords, starting with the B formation C chord:

C Chords

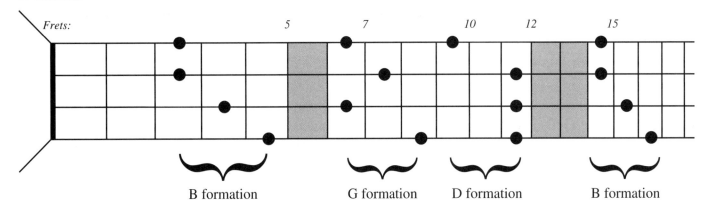

Here's the G–D–B roadmap with 7th chords. It includes a fourth moveable seventh chord, based on a first position F7:

C7 Chords

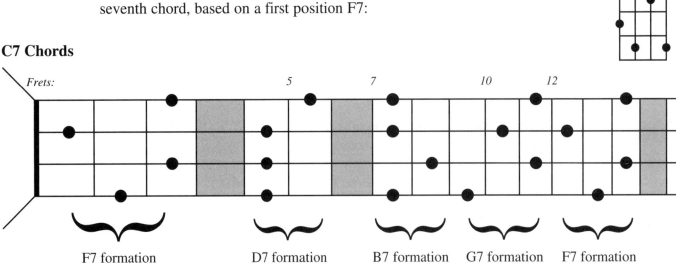

Here's the G–D–B roadmap with minor chords.

Gm Chords

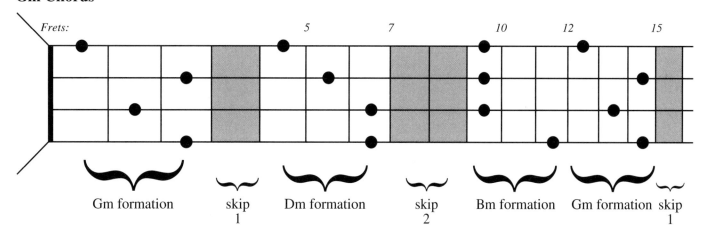

DO IT! **Practice the G–D–B roadmaps (major, minor, and 7th) by playing all the voicings of any one chord, going up and down the neck.** For example, strum a steady 4/4 rhythm and play all the G chords (one bar for each voicing), then all the G minor and G7th chords:

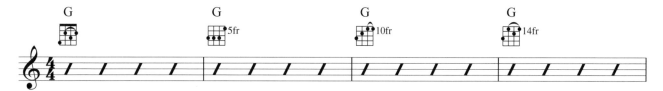

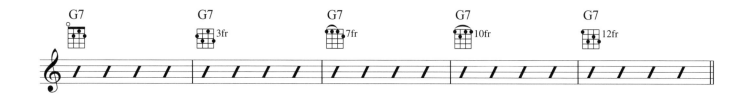

Play the following backup to the old folk song "Sloop John B." The tune lingers for several bars on each chord, giving you the opportunity to play several formations for every chord. This arrangement makes use of two banjo rolls from the Preliminaries section: the forward roll (in the first eight bars) and the forward-backward roll (in the last eight bars).

SLOOP JOHN B.

Use the G–D–B chords to play a solo to the country standard "Wabash Cannonball." Instead of stating the melody, this solo is an improvisation based on ascending and descending chord formations.

WABASH CANNONBALL

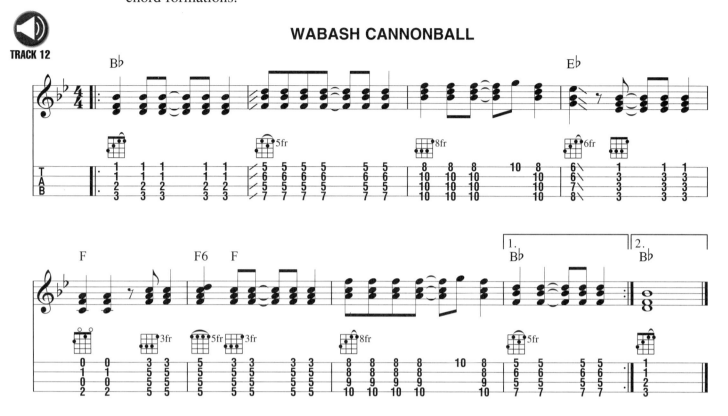

Use the minor G–D–B roadmap when playing backup chords to the Russian folk tune "Meadowlands."

MEADOWLANDS

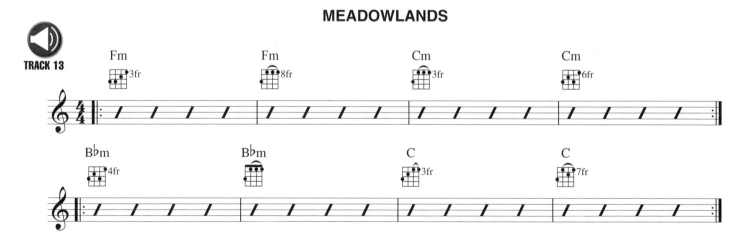

Use the 7th chord G–D–B roadmap to play backup for the blues tune "Betty and Dupree." In blues songs, it's not unusual for all the chords to be 7ths.

BETTY AND DUPREE

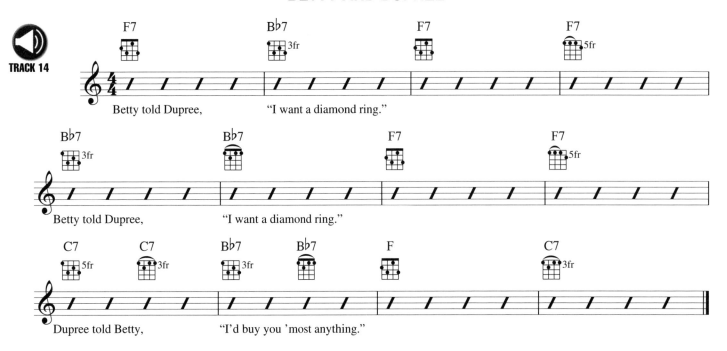

TRACK 14

Betty told Dupree,   "I want a diamond ring."

Betty told Dupree,   "I want a diamond ring."

Dupree told Betty,   "I'd buy you 'most anything."

SUMMING UP—NOW YOU KNOW...

1. How to use the three moveable major chords to play any major chord all over the fretboard.

2. How to use the three moveable minor chords to play any minor chord all over the fretboard.

3. How to use four moveable 7th chords to play any 7th chord all over the fretboard.

CHORD FRAGMENT/ CHORD FAMILIES

Three B Chord Families:

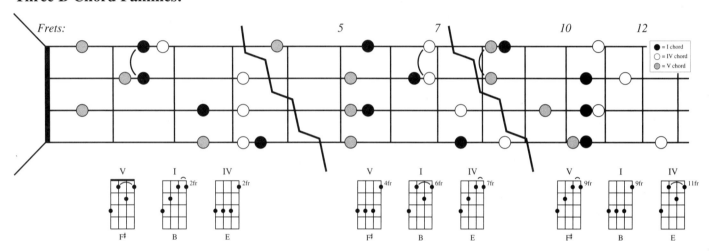

WHY? It's easier to learn new tunes and create solos or play backup when you understand chord families and know how to play them all over the fretboard. **ROADMAP #7** arranges the three moveable major chords (G, D, and B formations) into chord families. It helps you hear common chord changes and play them automatically.

WHAT? **Every song has a chord progression**—a repeated chord sequence in which each chord is played for a certain number of bars.

Thousands of tunes consist of just three chords: the I, IV, and V chords. These three chords are a "chord family." "I," "IV," and "V" refer to steps of the major scale of your key.

- The I chord is the key center. In the key of C, C is the I chord because C is the first note in the C major scale.
- The IV chord is the chord whose root is the fourth note in the major scale of your key. In the key of C, F is the IV chord, since F is the fourth note in the C major scale.
- The V chord is the chord whose root is the fifth note in the major scale of your key. In the key of C, G is the V chord, since G is the fifth note in the C scale.

ROADMAP #7 shows three ways of playing the "key of B" chord family: with a B-formation I chord, a G-formation I chord, and a D-formation I chord.

The relationships in ROADMAP #7 are moveable. Once you learn them, you can make chord changes automatically. For example, in any key, if you're playing a *I chord* with a B formation, the *V chord* is the G formation a fret lower.

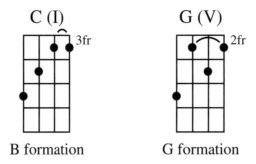

C (I)   G (V)

B formation   G formation

HOW? **Practice playing different chord families, combining ROADMAPS #7 and #6, the G–D–B ROADMAP.** For example, here are three key-of-G chord families:

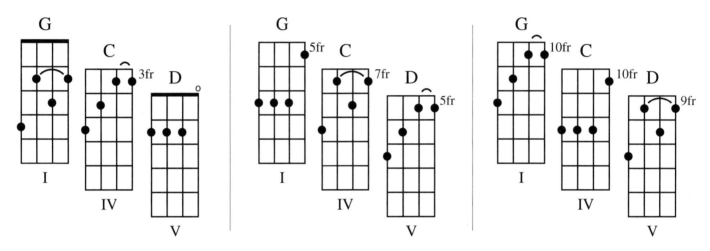

Strum the following progression, in many keys, all over the fretboard. It fits a number of well-known tunes, including "Louie Louie," "La Bamba," "Wild Thing," "Twist and Shout," and "Good Lovin'," so hum one of those tunes while you strum! It'll help you get so familiar with the I–IV–V chord relationships that they'll become automatic—especially if you do this all over the fretboard in different keys and keep a steady rhythm while you're strumming.

For example, in C:

TRACK 15

‖: I   IV | V   IV :‖

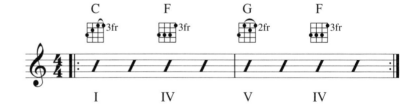

Learn to recognize the sound of a V chord and a IV chord. Here's a good exercise to help you do this:

- Strum any chord four times (C at the 3rd fret, for example).
- Keeping a steady rhythm, strum its V chord (G at the 2nd fret) four times.
- Do this with many different chords, all over the uke, until you recognize the "sound" of going from I to V.
- Repeat the same process all over the uke, this time going from I to IV.

DO IT! **Play "Midnight Special" to practice memorizing the chord family relationships.** While you're strumming it, be aware you're playing this progression: I–IV–I–V–I.

MIDNIGHT SPECIAL

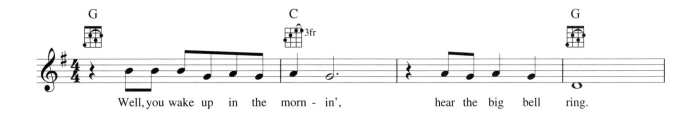

Well, you wake up in the morn - in', hear the big bell ring.

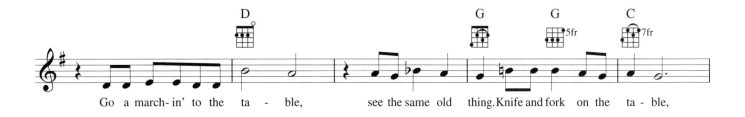

Go a march-in' to the ta - ble, see the same old thing. Knife and fork on the ta - ble,

noth - in' in my pan. If you say a word a - bout it,

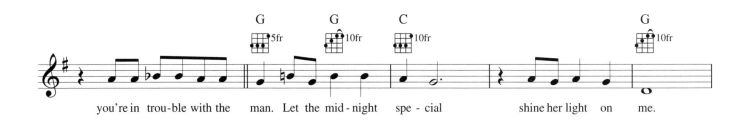

you're in trou-ble with the man. Let the mid-night spe - cial shine her light on me.

Let the mid-night spe - cial shine her ev - er-lov-in' light on me.

Play the following cowboy song, "Streets of Laredo," in E♭. As you play it, be aware of which chords are I (E♭), IV (A♭), and V (B♭). Then try playing it in other keys.

STREETS OF LAREDO

I, IV, and V are the only chords you need to play a 12-bar blues. This famous chord progression is the basis of countless blues, rock, country, bluegrass, and swing tunes. Some famous songs with the 12-bar blues format include "Stormy Monday," "Route 66," "Hound Dog," "Whole Lotta Shakin' Goin' On," "Shake, Rattle, and Roll," "Johnny B. Goode," and "Kansas City." There are lots of variations of the 12-bar blues, but here's the basic pattern in G:

Key of G:

‖: G | ⁄ | ⁄ | ⁄ | C | ⁄ | G | ⁄ | D | ⁄ | G | ⁄ :‖
  I   IV   I   V   I

Each of the twelve bars (measures) in the above blues progression has four beats. The repeat sign (⁄) means "repeat the previous bar."

"Hesitation Blues," below, goes back nearly a century. After playing it, strum it again and hum any of the other blues tunes mentioned above.

HESITATION BLUES

The V chord is always two frets above the IV chord and vice versa (the IV chord is always two frets below the V chord). That means you have alternative ways to play your I–IV–V chord families:

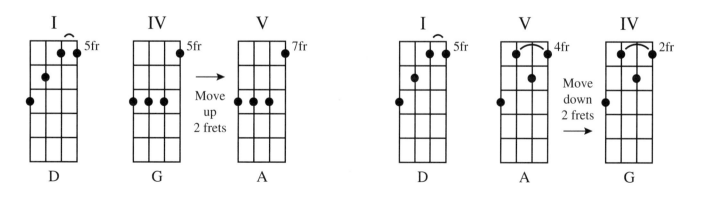

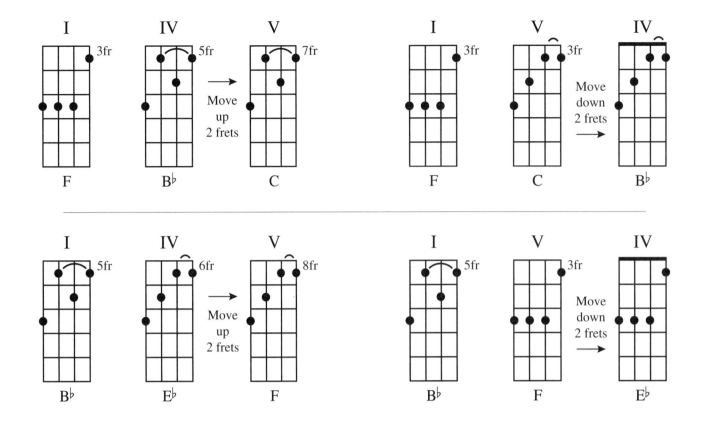

The gospel tune "Oh Mary, Don't You Weep" makes use of these alternate IV and V chords:

OH MARY, DON'T YOU WEEP

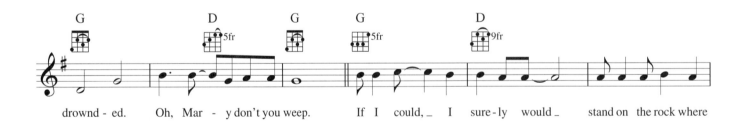

Oh, Mar-y don't you weep, don't you mourn, oh, Mar-y don't you weep, don't you mourn. Pha-roah's ar – my got

drownd-ed. Oh, Mar – y don't you weep. If I could, _ I sure-ly would _ stand on the rock where

Mo-ses stood. _ Pha-roah's ar – my got drownd-ed. Oh, Mar – y don't you weep.

You can re-map the I–IV–V chord families with 7th and 9th chords. This enables you to enhance your blues backup, since blues tunes are often composed of 7th or 9th chords instead of major chords. Here are the B chord families, converted to 7th and 9th chords, followed by a bluesier version of "Hesitation Blues."

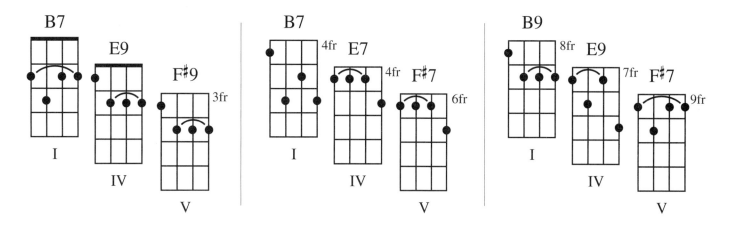

HESITATION BLUES
(with 7ths and 9ths)

SUMMING UP—NOW YOU KNOW...

1. How to locate three different chord families for any key using major or 7th chords.

2. How to use all three chord families to play tunes using major or 7th chords.

3. An alternate way to locate IV and V chords.

4. The meanings of these musical terms:
   a) I Chord
   b) IV Chord
   c) V Chord
   d) Chord Family
   e) 12-Bar Blues

CHORD SOLOING

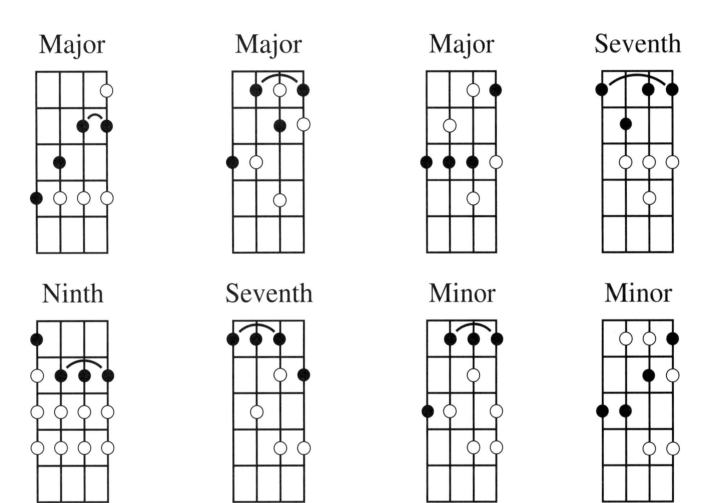

WHY? Uke players can do more than strum an accompaniment; they can play songs just like a pianist or guitarist, in the form of chord solos—chords and melody at the same time. Learn how to vary your moveable chords à la **ROADMAP #8** and you'll be able to play instrumental solos on the uke in addition to (or instead of) strumming backup.

WHAT? **To play chord-melody solos, strum the chord voicing whose top (highest) note is the melody note.** The idea is to put the melody on the first or second string, where it stands out, and to harmonize it with the other notes in the chord. (Due to the unique "My Dog Has Fleas" tuning of the uke, melody notes may also be played on the high fourth string.)

You don't need a chord for every melody note. It's sufficient to play a chord with the first note of a melodic phrase.

Play a chord with every chord change that occurs, whether it's at the beginning or in the middle of a melodic phrase. By this standard, you wind up playing one or two chords per bar of music.

Each chord shape in ROADMAP #8 is surrounded by circled notes that can be played with the basic chord formation. If the melody note is not in the basic chord shape, it's probably one of these extra notes. Sometimes you can add a circled note with a spare fretting finger; sometimes you change fingering to flat a note.

You've seen the chord grids of **ROADMAP #8** in Chapters 3, 4, and 5. You can use any of the major, minor, and 7th chords in those chapters to play chord solos; these are some of the most useful shapes.

You can also follow a song's chord progression and ad lib solos by playing chord-based licks.

HOW?

Play the following chord-based licks. Keep your left hand loosely in the pictured chord position. These samples show how you can play chords and melody at the same time.

TRACK 21

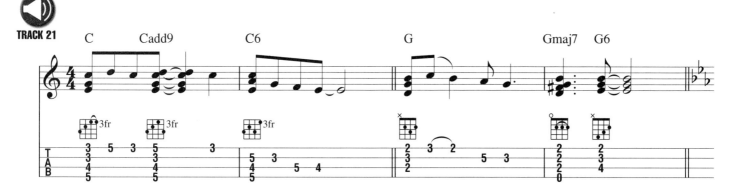

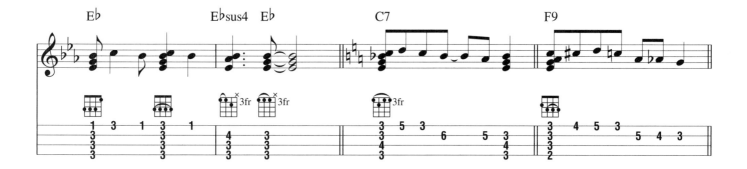

First position chords (chords that include open strings) can also be used in chord solos. The "extra notes" of **ROADMAP #8** can be applied to first positions chords if you relate each one to its equivalent moveable chord. Lower each of the following moveable chords one fret and you get a familiar first position chord:

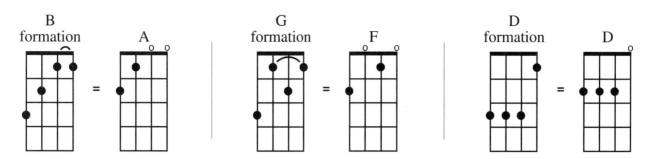

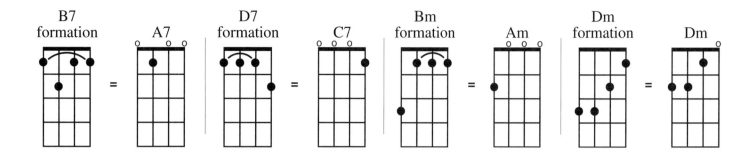

DO IT! Here are some chord-melody solos for familiar tunes. As you play them, notice how you sometimes have to play a higher or lower voicing of a chord in order to reach a higher or lower melody note.

LITTLE BROWN JUG

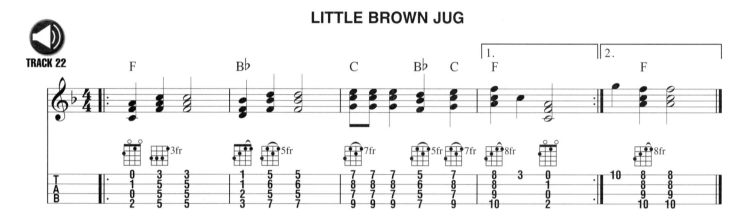

The following solo shows how to improvise with chord-based licks. It's an improvisation based on "Little Brown Jug." Jazz players usually state the melody of a tune (as in the previous arrangement) and then make up solos based on the song's chord progression, like this:

LITTLE BROWN JUG (Ad Lib)

Play this chord solo for "Aura Lee," the old folk song that was the basis for Elvis Presley's "Love Me Tender."

AURA LEE

TRACK 24

Here's a chord-melody arrangement of "Hesitation Blues," which you played in the previous chapter.

HESITATION BLUES

TRACK 25

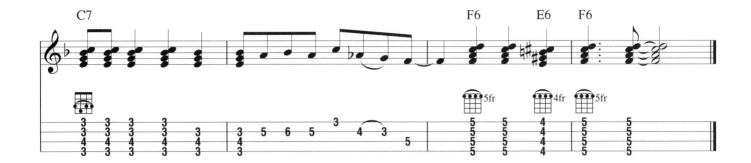

SUMMING UP—NOW YOU KNOW...

1. How to base licks and solos on moveable chord formations.

2. How to play a chord-melody solo using moveable chords and chord-based licks.

3. How to improvise, chord-style, over a chord progression.

FIRST POSITION MAJOR SCALES

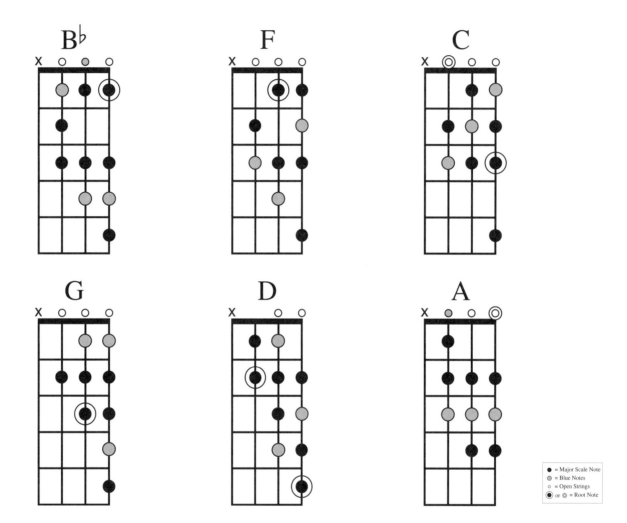

WHY? It's easier to play a song's melody or improvise a solo when you're familiar with major scales.

WHAT? **Every key has its own scale and characteristic licks.** You use the C scale to play in the key of C, the E scale to play in E, and so on.

Often, a scale (and the licks that go with it) can be played throughout a tune, in spite of chord changes within the tune.

A root is the note that gives the scale its name.

The root notes in each scale are circled.

The gray circles are "blue notes"—flatted 3rds, 5ths, and 7ths. They add a bluesy flavor to the scales.

44

HOW? Put your hand "in position" for each scale by fingering the appropriate chord (e.g., play an A chord to get in position for the A major scale). You don't have to maintain the chord while playing the scale, but it's a reference point.

Play up and down each scale until it feels comfortable and familiar. Play the chord before playing the scale and loop the scale—play it several times in a row, with no pause between repetitions. Here are the six easiest scales to practice:

B♭ Major Scale

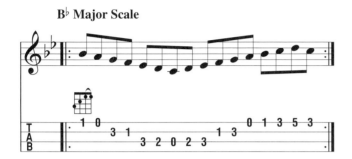

F Major Scale

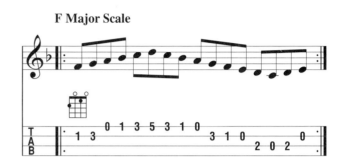

C Major Scale

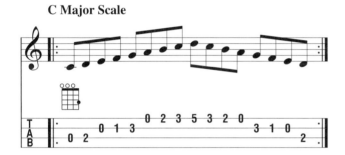

G Major Scale

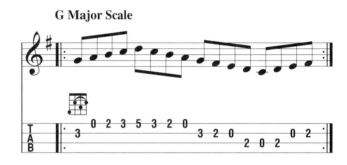

D Major Scale

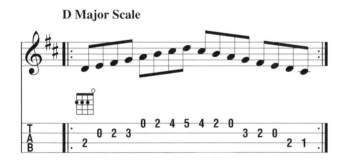

A Major Scale

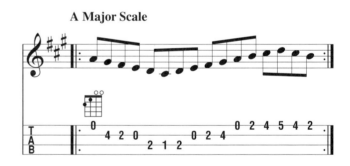

DO IT! **Try playing familiar melodies in several keys:**

- Play any major scale (C, for example).
- Strum a C chord to establish the key and, just using your ear, try to play the melody to "Twinkle Twinkle, Little Star." How hard could it be?
- Do the same steps in a different key.
- Do the same steps with a different tune.

Often, you can play tunes and ad lib melodies using the major scale that matches your key… especially if you add occasional blue notes. There's no need to change scales with every chord in the song! If you're playing a song in the key of C, you can probably play the melody using the C major scale. If you're jamming with another player who's playing chords (on another uke, guitar, piano, or accordion), you can improvise single-note solos using that same C scale.

The following single-note solos show how to use all six major scales to play a tune and decorate it with colorful licks. These improvisations are based on "Aloha Oe," the famous Hawaiian farewell song. Each solo shows how to embellish the song's melody, using major scales and adding occasional blue notes.

Listen to Track 26 to learn the basic melody of "Aloha Oe."

ALOHA OE—Basic Melody

ALOHA OE—B♭ Major Scale

ALOHA OE—F Major Scale

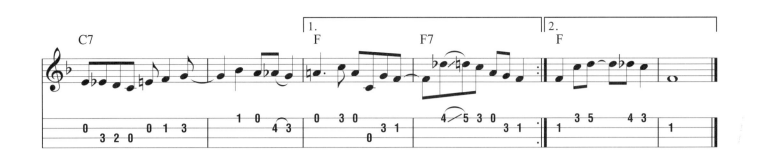

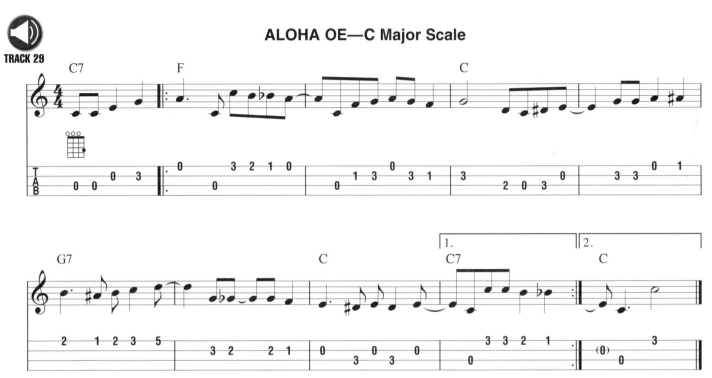

ALOHA OE—C Major Scale

TRACK 29

ALOHA OE—G Major Scale

TRACK 30

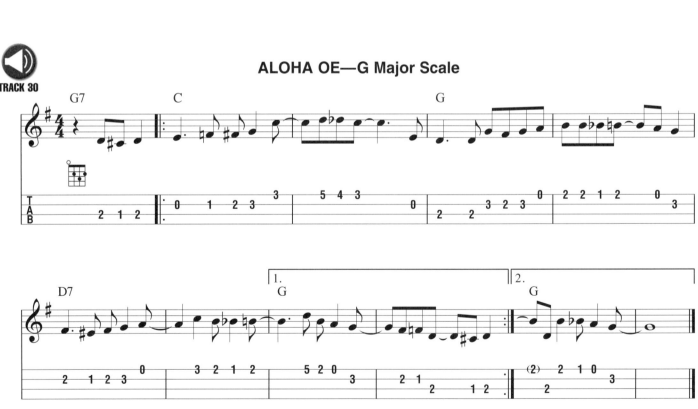

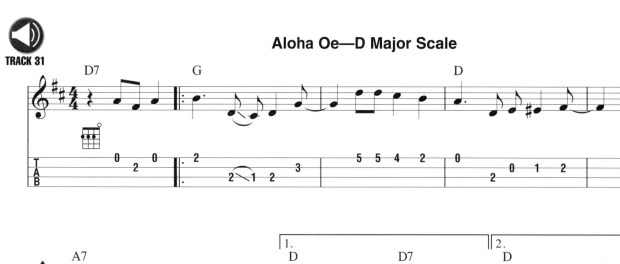

Aloha Oe—D Major Scale

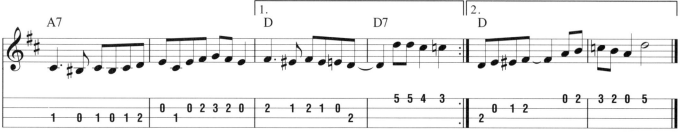

Aloha Oe—A Major Scale

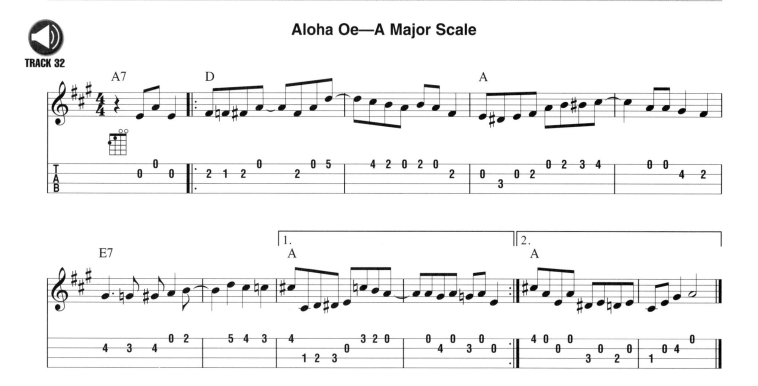

SUMMING UP—NOW YOU KNOW...

1. How to play six first-position major scales (B♭, F, C, G, D, and A) and how to use them to play licks and solos.

2. The meaning of the musical term "blue notes" and how to add them to your major scales and licks.

FOUR MOVEABLE MAJOR SCALES

G Scales

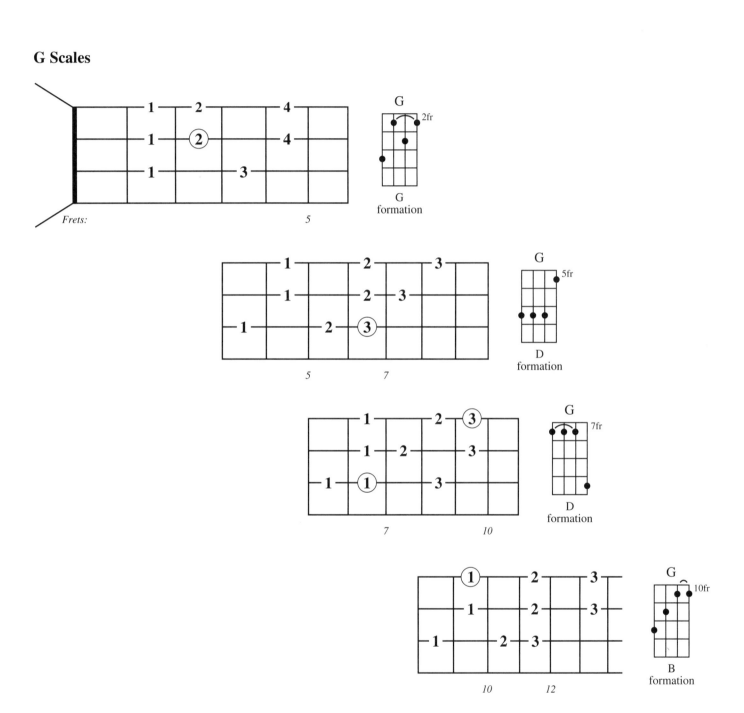

WHY? The moveable major scales help you play melodies and ad lib solos in any key, all over the fretboard. They bring you a step closer to any player's goal: to be able to play whatever you can hear.

WHAT?

The numbers on the fretboard in ROADMAP #10 are left-hand fingering suggestions.

The four scales of ROADMAP #10 are based on the chord shapes of ROADMAPS #3, 4, and 5 (the D, G, and B shapes). The root notes (Gs) are circled. Play the appropriate chord shape to get your fretting hand in position to play one of the major scales. For example, play a G formation at the 2nd fret to play the lowest G scale of ROADMAP #10.

Like the first position major scales of ROADMAP #9, **one moveable major scale can often be used to play a whole tune—both the melody and improvisation;** you don't have to change scales with each chord change. If a song is in the key of G, use the G major scale throughout.

HOW?

Here are the four G major scales that match the three G chord shapes. (There are two scales that match the D shape.) Play each chord shape before playing the scale. Start each scale with its root note so you can recognize the "do-re-mi" sound you have heard all your life!

G formation/ G Major Scale

D formation/ G Major Scale

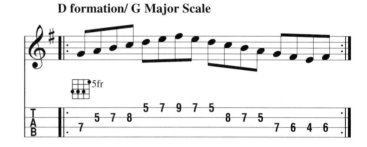

Second D formation/ G Major Scale

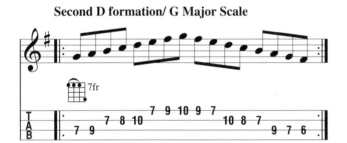

B formation/ G Major Scale

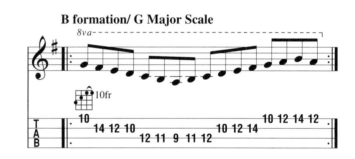

You can move the moveable major scales around, using the root notes to locate any scale you want. If a song is in C, you can use these four major scales:

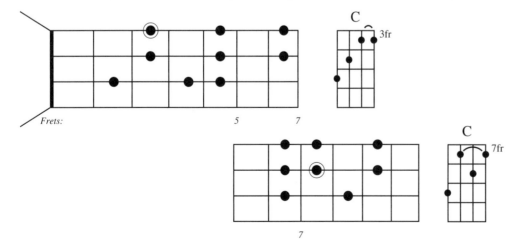

50

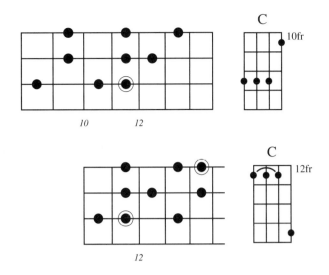

You can use the moveable major scales to play melodies and improvise solos, just as you did with the first position scales of **ROADMAP #9.** But now you can play in any key, and you can choose whether to play in a high, low, or medium register for each key.

DO IT!   **Use major scales to play melodies.** For example, here's the melody to "Buffalo Gals" in E♭. After playing it, try it again in E by moving everything up a fret; then do it again in D, moving it down a fret from the E♭ version.

TRACK 33

BUFFALO GALS—Melody in E♭, D formation

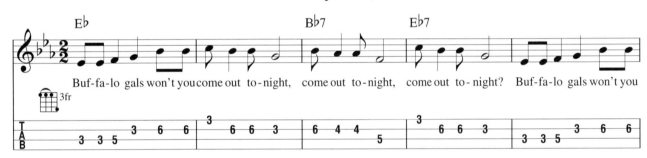

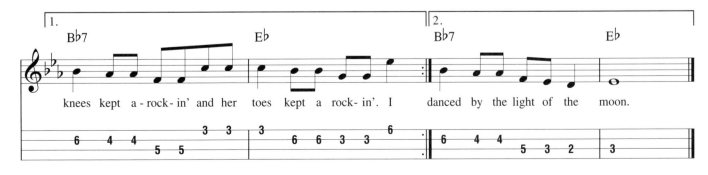

Use major scales to improvise solos. Soloists often ad lib melodies and licks over a familiar tune. For example, after playing the melody to "Buffalo Gals," you might improvise a solo over the same chord changes, using the same D formation major scale.

BUFFALO GALS—Ad lib Solo in E♭, D formation

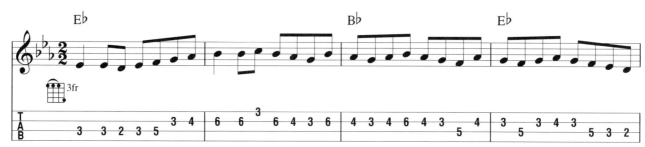

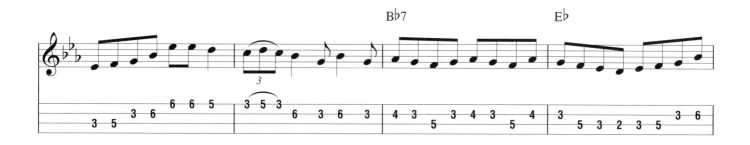

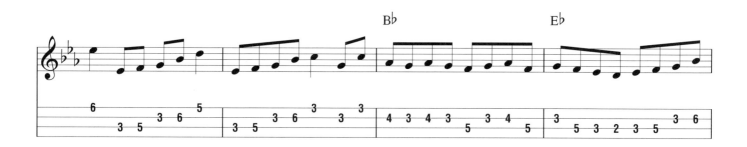

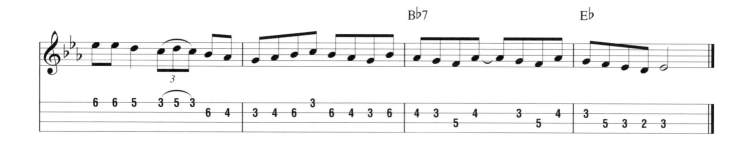

Here's "In the Good Old Summertime" in the key of B♭. As you did with "Buffalo Gals," play the arrangement below, then play it in different keys, using the same (B) formation: play it in C, D, and so on.

IN THE GOOD OLD SUMMERTIME—Melody in B♭, B formation

In the good old sum - mer time, in the good old sum - mer time,

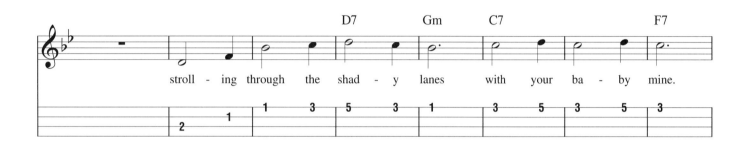

stroll - ing through the shad - y lanes with your ba - by mine.

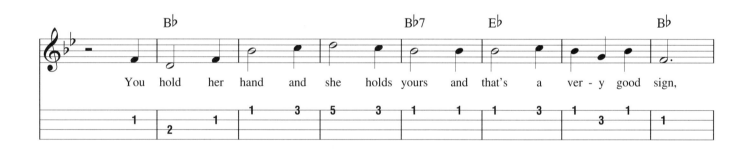

You hold her hand and she holds yours and that's a ver - y good sign,

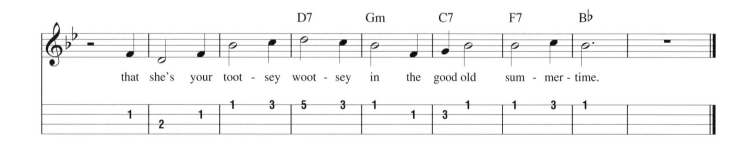

that she's your toot - sey woot - sey in the good old sum - mer - time.

"Oh, My Darling Clementine" makes use of the G-formation major scale. Play it as written, then move it up to A, B♭, etc.

TRACK 36

OH, MY DARLING CLEMENTINE—Melody in G, G formation

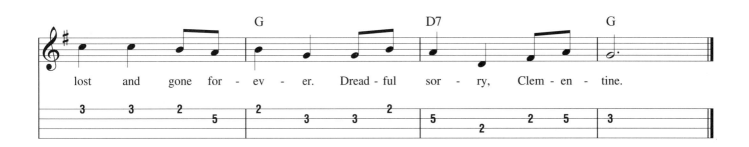

In addition to freely improvising, you can use major scales to ornament a given melody. Here's an ad lib solo to "Oh, My Darling Clementine." The melody is made fancier by the inclusion of "extra notes" from the G major scale. To create this type of embellishment, surround the sustained melody notes with scale increments. For example, if the melody has a sustained G note:

- play G–F♯–E–F♯–G (dipping below the melody note and coming back to it), or
- play G–A–B–A–G (going above the melody note and coming back to it), or
- play G–F♯–G–A–G (circling around the melody note).

TRACK 37

OH, MY DARLING CLEMENTINE—Ornamented Melodic Solo in G, G formation

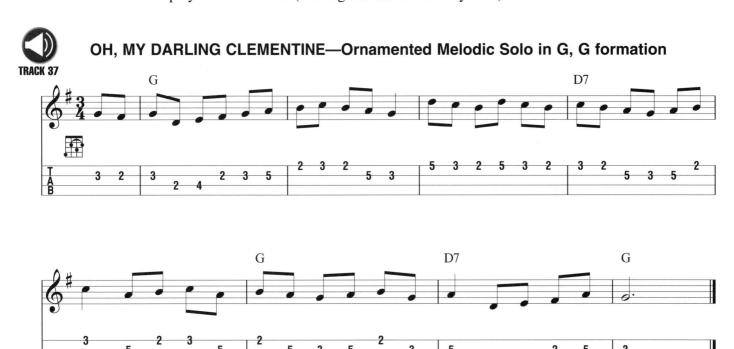

Some songs have such a wide range that it takes two scale positions to play them:

AVALON—Melody in G, G formation and D formation

TRACK 38

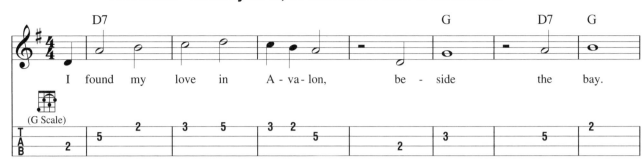

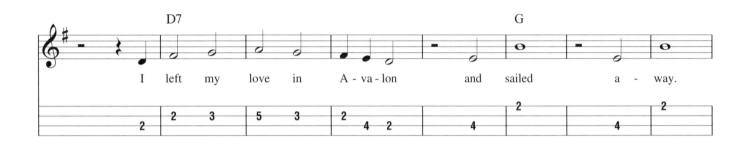

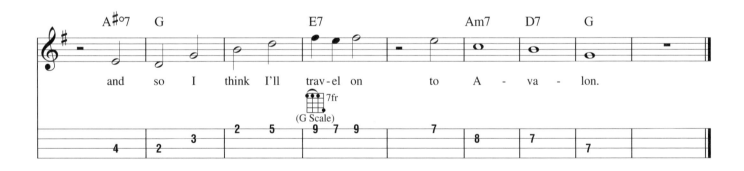

Many melodies include a few "accidentals": notes that are not in the major scale of their key. Familiarity with the major scale makes it easy to find these notes, as they're always one fret above or below the major scale notes. For example:

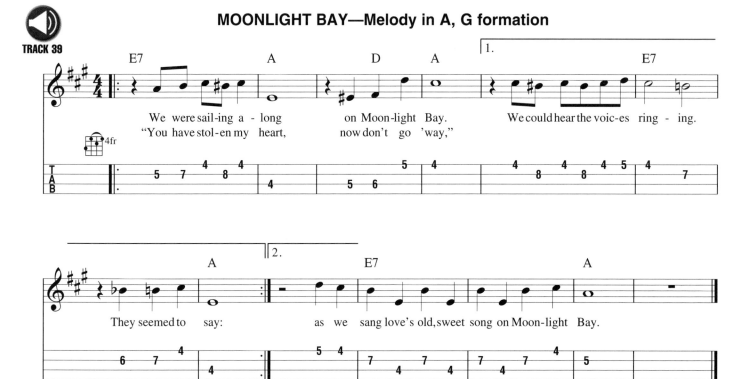

TRACK 39

MOONLIGHT BAY—Melody in A, G formation

We were sail-ing a - long   on Moon-light Bay.   We could hear the voic-es ring - ing.
"You have stol-en my heart,   now don't go 'way,"

They seemed to say: as we sang love's old, sweet song on Moon-light Bay.

SUMMING UP—NOW YOU KNOW...

1. How to play four moveable major scales for each key.

2. How to use them to play melodies.

3. How to use them to ornament a melody and ad lib solos.

4. The meaning of the musical term "accidental."

THE CIRCLE OF FIFTHS

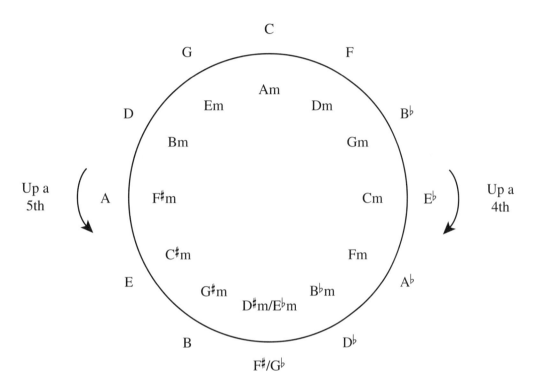

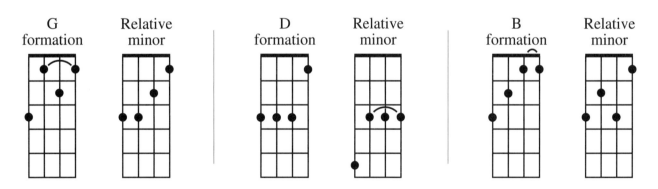

WHY? Many songs include more than just the I, IV, and V chords. These subtler chord progressions are easier to understand and play once you are acquainted with relative minors and circle-of-fifths movement.

WHAT? The circle of fifths (also called the circle of fourths) arranges the twelve musical notes so that **a step counterclockwise takes you up a 5th, and a step clockwise takes you up a 4th.**

- Counterclockwise: G is a 5th above C, B is a 5th above E, etc.

- Clockwise: F is a 4th above C, B♭ is a 4th above F, etc.

Every major chord has a relative minor chord that has many of the same notes as its relative major. The relative minor is the vi chord; A is the sixth note in the C major scale, so Am is the relative minor to a C major chord. Notice the similarities between the two chords. (The use of lower-case Roman numerals, as in the *vi chord*, indicates *minor chords*.)

Am is relative minor to C; C is relative major to Am.

If a song includes minor chords, they are usually the relative minors of the I, IV, and V chords. A song in the key of C might include Am (relative minor of C), Dm (relative minor of F, the IV chord), or Em (relative minor of G, the V chord).

The chord grids in ROADMAP #11 show how to alter each of the three moveable major chords to play its relative minor:

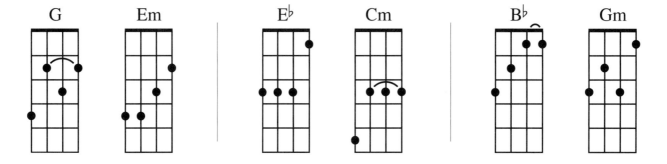

HOW? In circle-of-fifths progressions, you leave the I chord, creating tension, and you resolve the tension by using clockwise motion to come back to I, going up by 4ths until you reach "home" at the I chord. For example, in "Raggy Blues," which follows, you jump from C to the A7 chord (leaving the C chord family) and then get back to C by going clockwise along the circle: D7 is a 4th above A7, G7 is a 4th above D7, and C is a 4th above G7. Strum the progression using four downstrokes per bar. It resembles "Alice's Restaurant" and many other tunes, including Robert Johnson's "They're Red Hot" and Bob Wills' "Bring It on Down to My House, Honey."

RAGGY BLUES

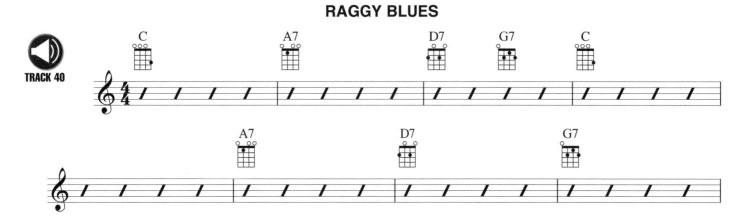

TRACK 40

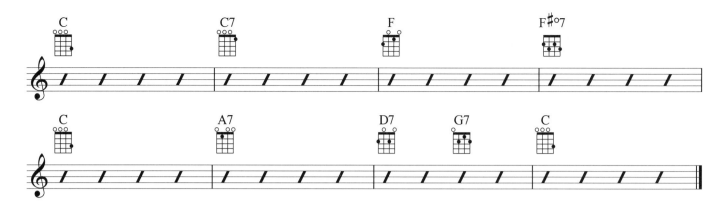

This is a I–VI–II–V progression, because A is a 6th above C, D is a 2nd above C, and G is a 5th above C.

As you move clockwise along the circle, **the chords can be major or minor, but the V chord is almost always a 7th.**

If you use moveable chords, refer back to ROADMAP #7 to remember how to move up a 4th:

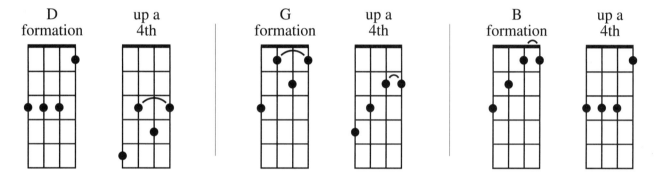

Do the same thing using 7th chords and minor chords:

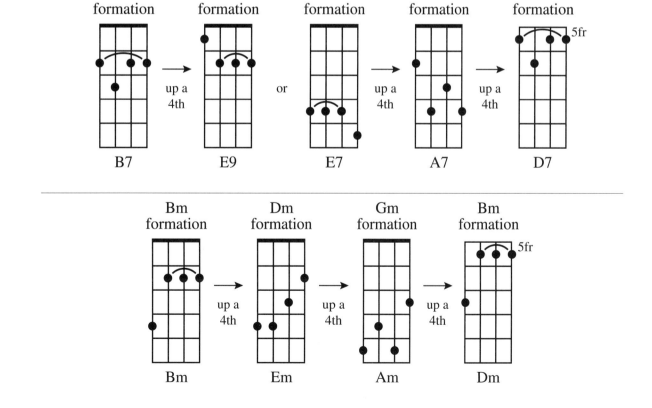

The I–VI–II–V often starts with a series of descending chords, taking you from I to VI. In fact, whenever you hear chords walking down three frets *chromatically* (one fret at a time), it usually means you're going from I to VI, starting a VI–II–V–I. It's the beginning of "Sweet Georgia Brown," "Up a Lazy River," "I Ain't Got Nobody," and many more:

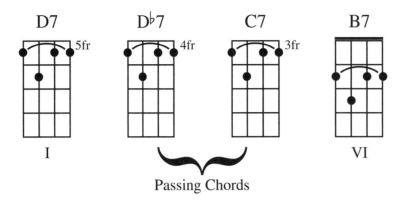

Passing Chords

Many songs contain a III–VI–II–V–I circle-of-fifths sequence. If it's in the bridge (a middle section of a tune, usually eight bars long) and the chords are all sevenths, it's referred to as the "I Got Rhythm" bridge. Notice how easy it is to play this progression, using two chord positions:

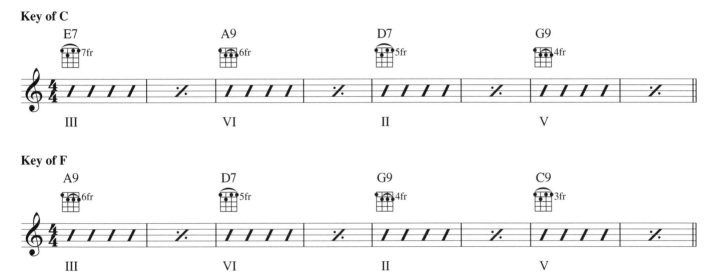

DO IT!

Play the I–vi–ii–V7 progression in many keys. This progression is so common that pros have nicknamed it "standard changes," the "dime store progression," "ice cream changes," "I Got Rhythm" changes (after the Gershwin song), or just "rhythm changes" for short. It's the basis for countless standards ("Blue Moon," "Heart and Soul," "These Foolish Things") and classic rock tunes ("Oh, Donna," "You Send Me," "Stand by Me," "Every Time You Go Away," "Every Breath You Take"). Try humming one of these songs while strumming this progression:

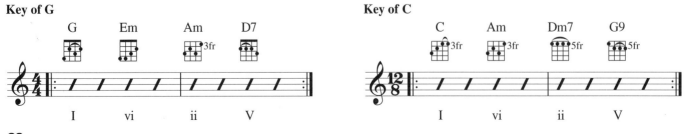

60

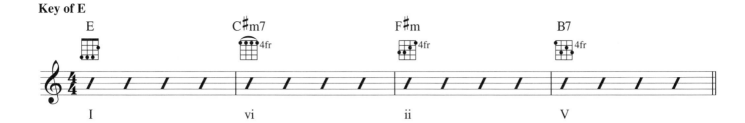

Key of E

Sometimes the IV chord is played instead of the minor ii chord. It's a small change because the IV chord is the relative major of ii. In the key of C, for example, Dm is ii, and F, its relative major, is IV.

Play VII–III–VI–II–V–I progressions, like "Mister Sandman" and "Red Roses for a Blue Lady." In these tunes, you jump halfway around the circle, from I (or C, in the key of C) to VII (B7); then you cycle back to C by going up a 4th (to E7), up another 4th (to A7), and so on, until you reach the C chord:

TRACK 43

Key of C

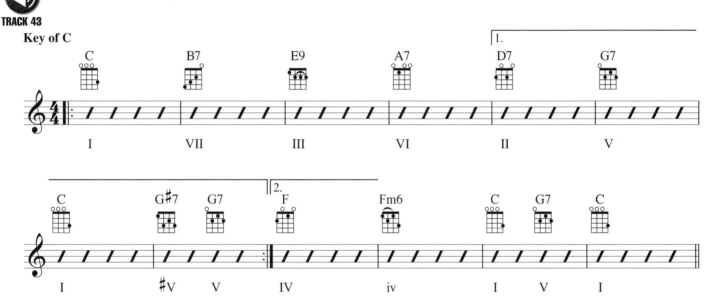

There's a standard circle-of-fifths eight-bar ending that appears in countless songs, including "All of Me," "Sit Right Down and Write Myself a Letter," "Pennies from Heaven," "Paper Doll," "On a Slow Boat to China," "Who's Sorry Now," "Mona Lisa," "It's a Sin to Tell a Lie," and more. Sing one of these eight-bar endings while strumming:

TRACK 44

Key of C

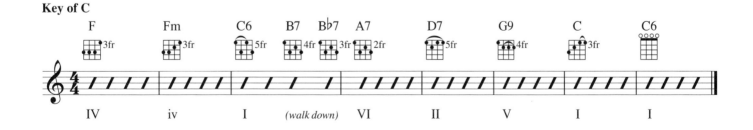

Play and analyze these two old jazz standards, which contain mostly circle-of-fifths chord movement. Strum and sing them along with the recording. Then study the progression in terms of intervals, noticing VI–II–V–I's and other patterns, and try playing them in other keys.

The Roman numerals between the music and grids are there to help you identify the chords   in terms of intervals and understand chord movement.

I USED TO LOVE YOU (BUT IT'S ALL OVER)

FOR ME AND MY GAL

TRACK 47

Make sure you can play typical circle of fifths-type chord changes, such as ii–V–I and I–vi–ii–V, in any key. These progressions occur in so many songs that it's important to memorize automatic, moveable ways of playing them. Strum these samples:

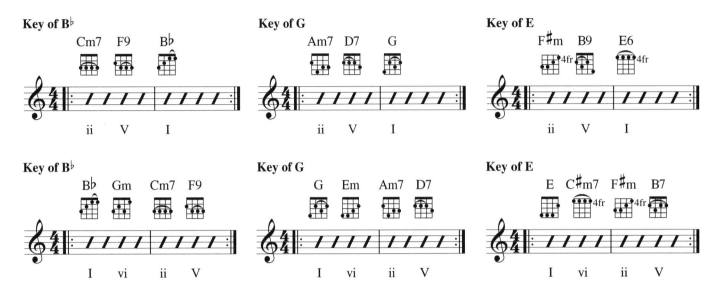

SUMMING UP—NOW YOU KNOW...

1. How to play several circle-of-fifths progressions in any key, including the "rhythm changes."

2. How to automatically find the relative minor of any moveable major chord.

3. How to automatically find the chord that is a fourth above any moveable major chord.

4. The meanings of these musical terms:
   a) Relative Minor
   b) Relative Major
   c) Chromatic
   d) Bridge, "I Got Rhythm" Bridge
   e) Rhythm Changes
   f) Standard Changes

MINOR PENTATONIC SCALES (THE BLUES BOX)

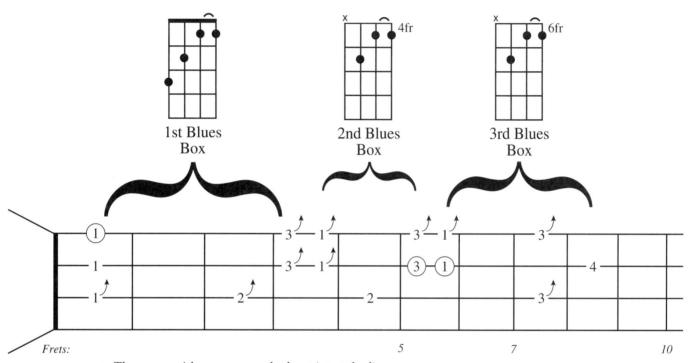

1st Blues Box   2nd Blues Box   3rd Blues Box

- *The notes with arrows can be bent (stretched).*
- *Each chord grid shows how to get your fretting hand "in position" for a blues box.*

WHY?   The moveable scales of this **ROADMAP**, often called *blues boxes*, are an invaluable tool for improvising single-note solos in nearly any popular music, including blues, rock, country, and jazz.

WHAT?   **The three blues boxes above are B♭ blues scales.** The root notes are circled. The numbers indicate suggested fingering positions.

Often, you can solo in one blues box throughout a song. Like the moveable major scales, blues boxes make it unnecessary to change scales with each chord change.

The blues boxes are pentatonic, which means they contain five notes. However, you can add other notes and still sound bluesy. The five notes are a good starting point.

HOW?

To put your left hand in position for the first blues box, play a B formation at the appropriate fret. For the key of B♭, play a B formation at the first fret, which is a B♭ chord.

First Blues Box, Key of B♭

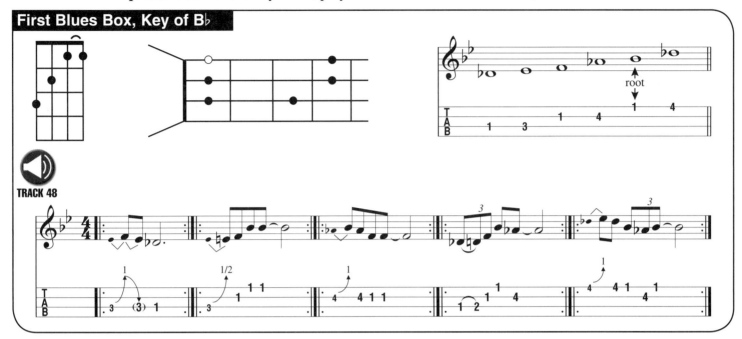

TRACK 48

To put your left hand in position for the second blues box, play the root note on the second string with your third (ring) finger. In B♭, play the B♭ note on the 2nd string, 6th fret, with your ring finger.

Second Blues Box, Key of B♭

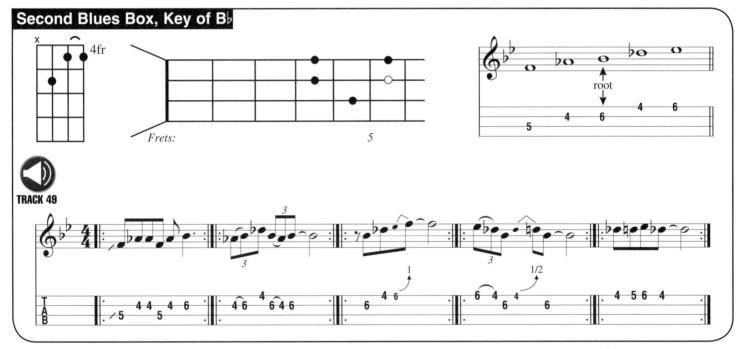

TRACK 49

To put your left hand in position for the third blues box, play the B formation of the IV chord.

Third Blues Box, Key of B♭

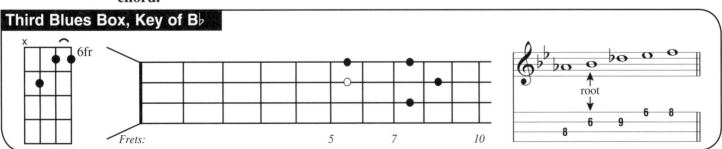

The third blues box is idiomatic; when blues players use it, they include notes that aren't part of the minor pentatonic scale:

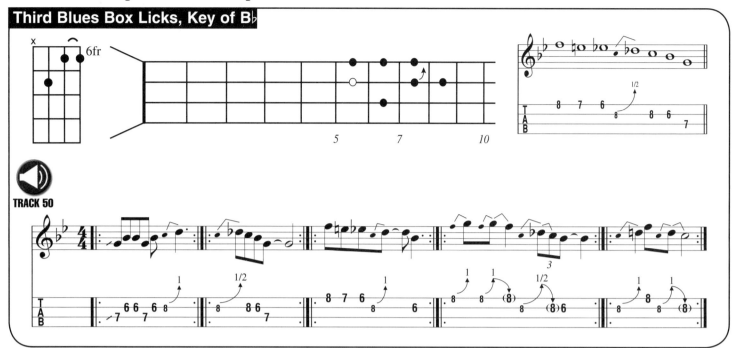

DO IT! **Use the blues boxes to solo on bluesy tunes.** In addition to blues tunes, that includes many rock, pop, country, and jazz songs—any song whose melody is based on the blues scale. If you play blues scale-based licks over a tune, your ear will tell you right away whether or not they sound appropriate.

The following solo illustrates the use of all three B♭ blues boxes in a typical jazzy 12-bar blues tune. It has the same flavor as "Route 66."

SOME OTHER ROUTE

In case you want to join a rock jam session, here's a typical garage-band chord progression in the key of A. The solo below uses all three A blues boxes. Since it's in A, the first box includes some open strings (it's what you get when you move the first B♭ blues box down a fret).

1st Blues Box, B♭

1st Blues Box, A

GARAGE BAND ROCK

TRACK 52

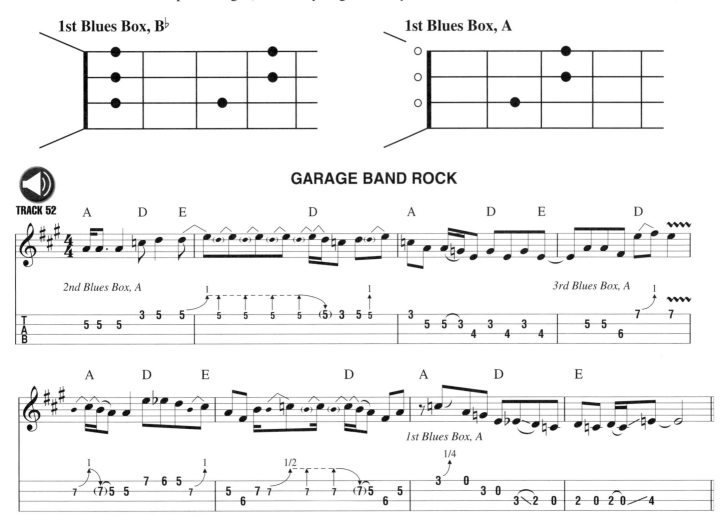

In some keys, if you try to use blues-box soloing, you quickly run out of frets. For example, if you play "Garage Band Rock" in G, the first blues box is way up at the 10th fret, and higher blues boxes are impractical on the uke. But you can play the 2nd and 3rd boxes *an octave lower* (12 frets lower), like this:

2nd Blues Box, key of G

Root

3rd Blues Box, key of G

Root

5

GARAGE BAND ROCK—in G

TRACK 53

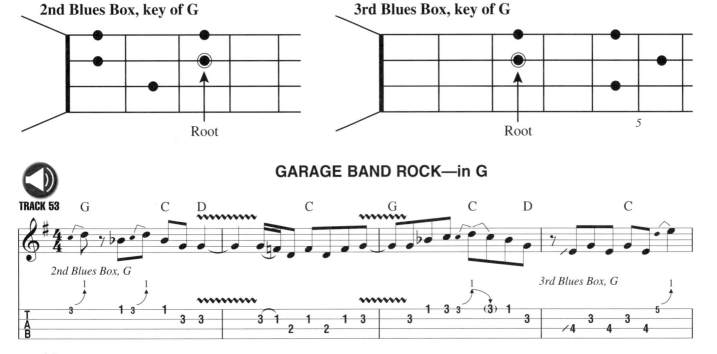

68

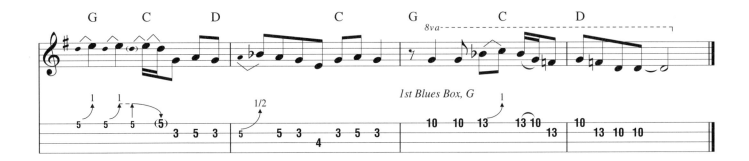

Often, the third blues box works well in non-bluesy tunes, where the first and second boxes sound inappropriate. "On the Beach at Waikiki," below, is about as far from a blues as you can get. It's in C, and the solo consists of licks in the third C blues box.

ON THE BEACH AT WAIKIKI

TRACK 54

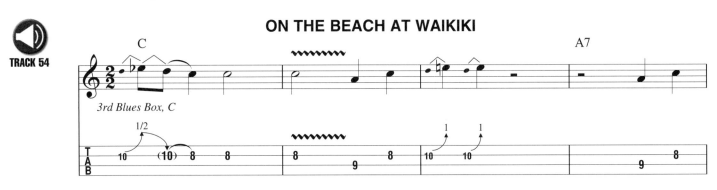

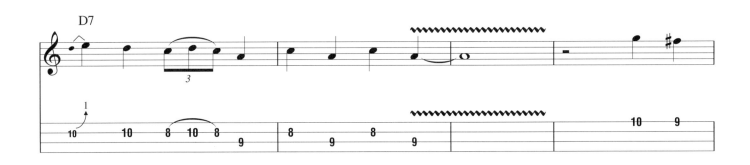

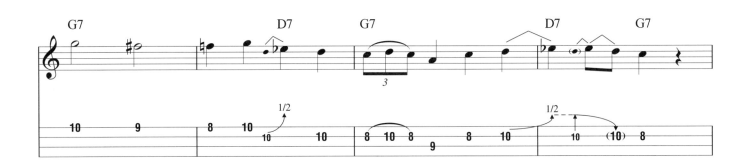

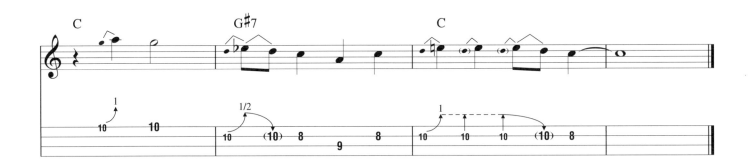

Relative minor blues scale substitution: When a song does not have a bluesy feel, you can still use the first and second blues boxes; just play them *three frets lower* than the song's actual key. For example, the following version of "The World Is Waiting for the Sunrise" is in the key of F, and the solo makes use of first and second D blues boxes.

THE WORLD IS WAITING FOR THE SUNRISE

SUMMING UP—NOW YOU KNOW...

1. Three moveable blues boxes.

2. Many licks that go with each box.

3. How to use the boxes to improvise single-note solos in any key.

4. How to substitute the relative minor blues scale when blues boxes don't fit in a tune.

TUNING CONVERSIONS

D Tuning and More

C tuning (GCEA) is the preferred tuning for most ukulele players today. It is also the accepted tuning for Hawaiian players. However, some prefer tuning their ukes a whole step higher to D tuning (A–D–F♯–B). Ukulele legend, Roy Smeck, was a D tuning player, favoring the brighter sound. Some tune a half step or two higher, to E♭ or E tuning.

D Tuning

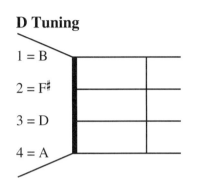

1 = B
2 = F♯
3 = D
4 = A

E♭ Tuning

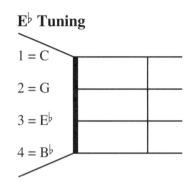

1 = C
2 = G
3 = E♭
4 = B♭

E Tuning

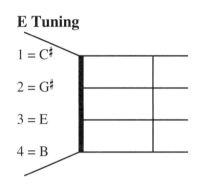

1 = C♯
2 = G♯
3 = E
4 = B

Reentrant Tuning

In C, D, and other tunings, most players like to tune *reentrant* style, which refers to the well-known "My Dog Has Fleas" melody. This means that the 4th string is higher than the lower-pitched 3rd string. Some players, including uke legend Herb Ohta (Ohta-San), like to tune the 4th string down an octave. The resulting lower string is handy if you are primarily an instrumentalist. It also makes uke chords more closely resemble guitar chords.

C Tuning (Non-Reentrant)

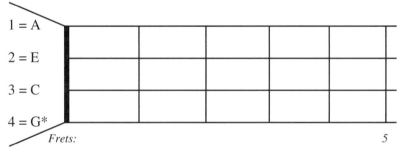

1 = A
2 = E
3 = C
4 = G*

Frets: 5

* The 4th string (G) is tuned an octave lower.

Baritone Uke G Tuning

The largest ukulele is the baritone; it is usually tuned a 4th lower than soprano, concert, or tenor ukes, to D–G–B–E, exactly like the highest four strings of the guitar. Baritones are rarely tuned reentrant.

Baritone Tuning (G6)

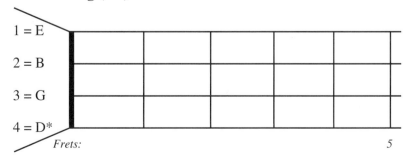

1 = E
2 = B
3 = G
4 = D*

Frets: 5

* The 4th string (D) is tuned an octave lower.

A Conversion Chart

When you play ukes tuned to D, G, or any other key, you use the familiar C-tuning chord shapes, but their names change. The following chart shows how to convert chords when playing on differently tuned ukes.

	C Tuning	D Tuning	G Tuning
C Major	C	C	C
D Major	D	D	D
E Major	E	E	E
F Major	F	F	F
G Major	G	G	G
A Major	A	A	A
B Major	B	B	B

Hints:

1. If a song is too high for you to sing, try playing baritone uke fingerings. This takes the key down a 4th.

2. D-tuning chords are a whole step higher than C-tuning chords. For example, the C-tuned F shape on a D-tuned uke forms a G chord (G is a whole step above F).

3. G-tuned uke chords are a 4th below C-tuned chords. For example, when you play the C-tuned F shape on a G-tuned uke, it's a C chord (C is a 4th below F).

USING THE PRACTICE TRACKS

The **ROADMAPS** in this book illustrate many backup and soloing styles, including:

- Strumming or picking many voicings of any one chord.
- Playing chord families "automatically."
- Single-note soloing based on moveable and first-position major scales.
- Single-note soloing based on blues boxes.
- Playing circle-of-fifths progressions "automatically."

On the four practice audio tracks, the uke is separated from the rest of the band—it's on one side of your stereo. You can tune it out and use the band as backup, trying out any soloing techniques you like. You can also imitate the recorded uke parts. Here are the soloing or backup ideas on each track.

#1 FRANKIE AND JOHNNY (in A, D, G, C, and F, in that order)

TRACK 56

This I–IV–I–V–I tune is played five times, in five different keys. The uke on one side of your stereo uses the first-position major scale of each key to play the melody, with some embellishment. The uke on the other side of the stereo strums rhythm with a small band. Here are a few practice ideas:

1. Play melody in all keys, using first position scales, and add some embellishments.

2. Ad lib single-note solos using first position and moveable scales.

3. Strum rhythm using first position chords, then moveable chords. Either way, you're practicing the use of I–IV–V chord families. Here's the 12-bar blues progression:

| I | ℅ | ℅ | ℅ | IV | ℅ | ℅ | I | V | ℅ | I | ℅ ||

#2 DOWN BY THE RIVERSIDE (in G)

TRACK 57

The track goes twice around this old gospel tune.

```
Verse:   | G  | ℅ | ℅ | ℅ | D7 | ℅ | G  | ℅ |
           I                   V       I
         | ℅ | ℅ | ℅ | ℅ | D7 | ℅ | G  | G7 ||
                               V       I

Chorus: ||: C  | ℅ | G  | ℅ | D7 | ℅ | G  | ℅ :||
           IV       I         V       I
```

Use this track to practice **ROADMAP #6**, the **G–D–B ROADMAP**. The song stays on one chord for several bars at a time, so you can shift from one voicing to another as you strum backup. For example, at the beginning of the tune, strum a first-position G for one bar, then the D formation G chord for one bar, then the B formation G chord for a bar, and so on.

#3 RUNNIN' WILD (in F and C)

TRACK 58 The uke plays blues scales throughout this thirty-two-bar standard. You can practice strumming along, using the chords below, to become familiar with the tune, then try your blues licks. The first time around the tune, the uke's solo is based on the three F blues boxes. The second time around, the song is in C and the uke's solo makes use of the A blues box (the substitute blues box), which is three frets below the C blues box.

Key of F:

```
|  F  |  ℅  |  F7 |  ℅  |  B♭ |  ℅  |  F  |  ℅  |
   I                     IV          I
|  C7 |  A7 |  Dm | B♭m |  C  |  G7 |  C7 |  ℅  ||
   V     III    vi    iv    V     II    V
|  F  |  ℅  |  F7 |  ℅  |  B♭ |  ℅  |  A7 |  D7 |
   I                     IV          III   VI
|  G7 |  C7 |  F  |  ℅  |  C7 |  ℅  |  F  |  ℅  ||
   II    V    I          V           I
```

Key of C:

```
|  C  |  ℅  |  C7 |  ℅  |  F  |  ℅  |  C  |  ℅  |
   I                     IV          I
|  G7 |  E7 |  Am |  Fm |  G  |  D7 |  G7 |  ℅  ||
   V     III   vi   iv    V     II    V
|  C  |  ℅  |  C7 |  ℅  |  F  |  ℅  |  E7 |  A7 |
   I                     IV          III   VI
|  D7 |  G7 |  C  |  ℅  |  G7 |  ℅  |  C  |  ℅  ||
   II    V    I          V           I
```

#4 TAKE ME OUT TO THE BALLGAME (in D and G)

TRACK 59 Use this classic tune to practice circle-of-fifths-type chord changes. Play it with first position chords, then try it using as many moveable chords as possible. Here are the chord changes in both keys. Intervals are written below the chord names to help you be aware of the VI–II–V–I progressions. Also notice the classic eight-bar ending that begins on the IV chord, as mentioned in the circle-of-fifths chapter. (Note: in this variation of the eight-bar ending, #IV° [C#°] is played, instead of iv [Cm].)

Key of D:

```
|  D  |  ℅  |  A7 |  ℅  |  D  |  ℅  |  A7 |  ℅  |
   I           V          I           V
|  B7 |  ℅  |  Em |  ℅  |  E9 |  ℅  |  A7 |  ℅  |
   VI          ii          II          V
|  D  |  ℅  |  A7 |  ℅  |  D7 |  ℅  |  G  |  ℅  |
   I           V          I           IV
|  ℅  | G#°7 |  D  |  B7 |  E9 |  A7 |  D  |  D7 ||
        #IV°    I    VI    II    V     I
```

Key of G:

```
|  G  |  ℅  |  D7 |  ℅  |  G  |  ℅  |  D7 |  ℅  |
   I           V          I           V
|  E9 |  ℅  |  Am |  ℅  |  A7 |  ℅  |  D9 |  ℅  |
   VI          ii          II          V
|  G  |  ℅  |  D7 |  ℅  |  G7 |  ℅  |  C  |  ℅  |
   I           V          I           IV
|  ℅  | C#°7 |  G  |  E9 |  A7 |  D7 |  G  |  ℅  ||
        #IV°    I    VI    II    V     I
```

CHORD DICTIONARY

Moveable Chords

This chord dictionary offers several different moveable chord formations for each chord type. The chord shapes can all be found in chapters 3, 4, and 5, but in this format you don't have to flip through pages to find them. The root of each formation is circled, *so if you know where the notes are up and down the fretboard,* you can play any chord several different ways. If the root is not included in the formation, a blank circle is written, indicating where the root is, in relation to the chord shape. (Don't play those blank circles; they are just there to show you where to place the chord on the fretboard.) The *interval formula* is written for each chord type (e.g., major chord = 1, 3, 5).

That brings up an interesting question: with only four notes per chord on the uke, how can you adequately express subtle chords like thirteenths or elevenths? The answer is that you have to pick the most important notes in the chord formula and skip the rest. Here are some tips:

1. Often, the root is expendable, as is the 5th.

2. If the chord is a seventh, the flatted 7th note must be included.

3. You also need the 3rd to make the minor or major part of the chord audible.

4. The "upper" intervals of a chord are essential. For example, if a chord is a 9th, 11th, or 13th, it will only sound like its namesake if it contains that high note: the 9th, 11th, or 13th.

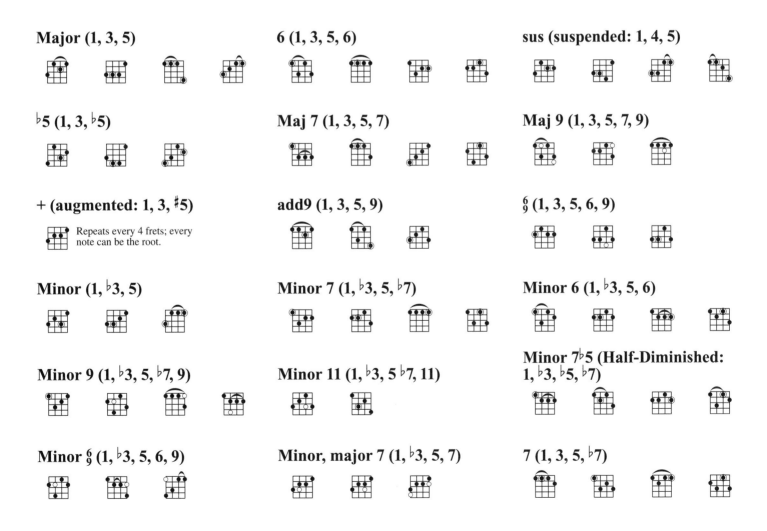

Major (1, 3, 5)

6 (1, 3, 5, 6)

sus (suspended: 1, 4, 5)

♭5 (1, 3, ♭5)

Maj 7 (1, 3, 5, 7)

Maj 9 (1, 3, 5, 7, 9)

+ (augmented: 1, 3, ♯5)

Repeats every 4 frets; every note can be the root.

add9 (1, 3, 5, 9)

⁶⁄₉ (1, 3, 5, 6, 9)

Minor (1, ♭3, 5)

Minor 7 (1, ♭3, 5, ♭7)

Minor 6 (1, ♭3, 5, 6)

Minor 7♭5 (Half-Diminished: 1, ♭3, ♭5, ♭7)

Minor 9 (1, ♭3, 5, ♭7, 9)

Minor 11 (1, ♭3, 5 ♭7, 11)

Minor ⁶⁄₉ (1, ♭3, 5, 6, 9)

Minor, major 7 (1, ♭3, 5, 7)

7 (1, 3, 5, ♭7)

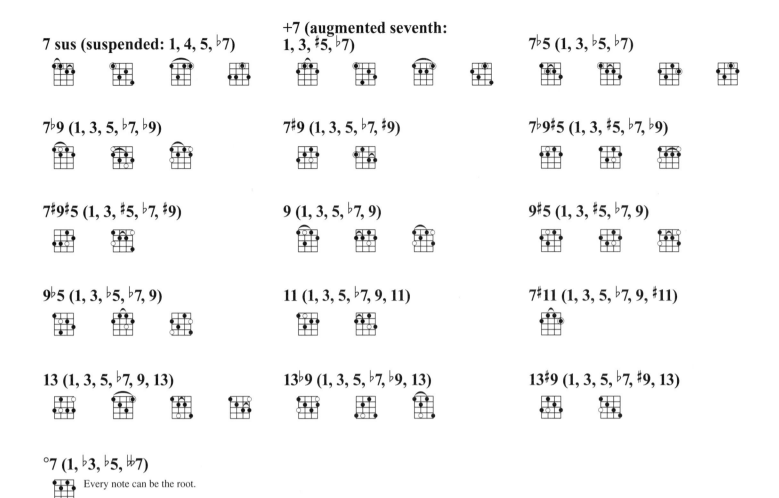

First Position Chords

Here are the first-position chords (chords that include open strings and are therefore not moveable) used in this book. Many of them are related to moveable chords. For example, if you move the first position D up a fret, you have to raise the open A on the 1st string by a fret as well; the result is the moveable D chord formation.

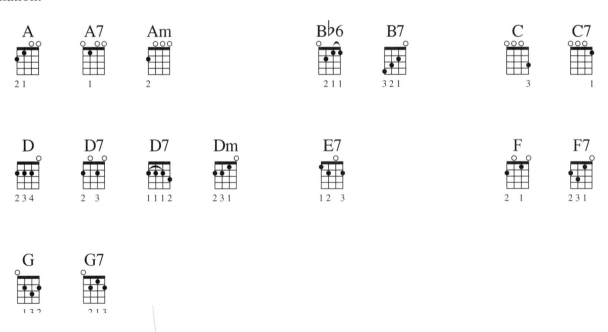

LISTENING SUGGESTIONS

The ukulele has enjoyed three major periods of popularity on the US mainland. The first occurred in 1915 thanks to the Panama Pacific Exposition in San Francisco. The Hawaiian pavilion at this early "world's fair" introduced many to the enchanting beauty of Hawaiian music and the ukulele. By the 1920s, the uke had become a necessary appendage for the college student, and numerous popular singers like Cliff "Ukulele Ike" Edwards played the Tin Pan Alley songs of the day on ukes. The second era was in the fifties and is largely credited to Arthur Godfrey who was never far from a uke on his very popular TV and radio shows. The current "third wave" began in the early 1990s thanks to a new generation of artists, ukulele songbook publishers, and the internet.

Fortunately, more and more vintage ukulele recordings are being re-released on CD these days. Although you may have to search a bit, recordings are available from all of these ukulele artists.

Hawaiian Pioneers:
Ernest Kaai—early virtuoso and one of the first ukulele instructional book authors/publishers.
Jesse Kalima—developed and popularized chord soloing technique.
Eddie Kamae—mentor to Herb Ohta and founder of the legendary "Sons Of Hawaii."
Herb Ohta (Ohta-San)—has recorded over 80 albums of ukulele instrumental music, and is a superstar in Hawaii and Japan.

US Mainland pioneers:
Cliff Edwards "Ukulele Ike"—a great singer, actor, and strummer. He introduced "Singin' in the Rain" on Broadway in 1929 and was the voice of Jiminy Cricket in Pinocchio.
Roy Smeck—a brilliant technician who used lots of novelty strums and moves in his vaudeville act as "The Wizard of the Strings."
Arthur Godfrey—baritone uke-playing radio and TV personality who revived the instrument in the early 1950s.
Lyle Ritz—the first to introduce the ukulele as a serious jazz instrument with his *How About Uke* LP for Verve in the late fifties.

Noteworthy "Third Wave" Artists (Hawaii):
Troy Fernandez—ukulele player of the Ka'au Crater Boys who lit up a new generation of uke fans and players in the early nineties.
Israel Kamakawiwo'ole—the uke player/singer whose heartfelt arrangement of "Over the Rainbow/What a Wonderful World" continues to be used in commercials, movies, and television shows.
Jake Shimabukuro—the most exciting uke player at the moment, he combines rock star moves with masterful speed and accuracy.
Other notable artists include **Herb Ohta Jr., Bryan Tolentino, Daniel Ho,** and **Brittni Paiva.**

Noteworthy "Third Wave" Artists (US Mainland):
There are many uke players on the US Mainland who are releasing their own CDs. Stylistically, these recordings cover the spectrum from new arrangements of old Tin Pan Alley songs to jazz, western swing, novelty, modern rock, and even classical music. Notable artists/groups include **Bag End Boys, Jim Beloff, Ukulele Dick, Ukulele Eck, Michelle Kiba, John King, Janet Klein, King Kukulele, Deb Porter, Estelle Reiner, Dan Sawyer, Shorty Long, Songs from a Random House, Bill Tapia, Ian Whitcomb,** and **Lil' Rev.**

Noteworthy "Third Wave" Artists (World):
The **Langley Ukulele Ensemble** is a high school group from Langley, British Columbia, who have released many recordings over their twenty-five year history. **James Hill** began his uke-playing career as a member of the Langley ensemble. He has released three highly-regarded solo albums that show off his impressive speed, accuracy, and touch. The **Ukulele Orchestra of Great Britain** has released a number of fun CDs where they cheekily tackle very un-ukulele-type material to often brilliant effect. Other notable artists include **Azo Bell** (Australia), **IWAO** (Japan), **The Ukulele Club De Paris** (France), **Ralph Shaw** (Canada), and **Manitoba Hal** (Canada).

UKULELE NOTATION LEGEND

THE MUSICAL STAFF shows pitches and rhythms and is divided by bar lines into measures. Pitches are named after the first seven letters of the alphabet.

TABLATURE graphically represents the ukulele fingerboard. Each horizontal line represents a a string, and each number represents a fret.

2nd string, 3rd fret   1st & 2nd strings open, played together   open F chord

HALF-STEP BEND: Strike the note and bend up 1/2 step.

WHOLE-STEP BEND: Strike the note and bend up one step.

GRACE NOTE BEND: Strike the note and immediately bend up as indicated. The first note does not take up any time.

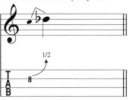

SLIGHT (MICROTONE) BEND: Strike the note and bend up 1/4 step.

BEND AND RELEASE: Strike the note and bend up as indicated, then release back to the original note. Only the first note is struck.

PRE-BEND: Bend the note as indicated, then strike it.

VIBRATO: The string is vibrated by rapidly bending and releasing the note with the fretting hand.

HAMMER-ON: Strike the first (lower) note with one finger, then sound the higher note (on the same string) with another finger by fretting it without picking.

PULL-OFF: Place both fingers on the notes to be sounded. Strike the first note and without picking, pull the finger off to sound the second (lower) note.

LEGATO SLIDE: Strike the first note and then slide the same fret-hand finger up or down to the second note. The second note is not struck.

SHIFT SLIDE: Same as legato slide, except the second note is struck.

TRILL: Very rapidly alternate between the notes indicated by continuously hammering on and pulling off.

TREMOLO PICKING: The note is picked as rapidly and continuously as possible.

NOTE: Tablature numbers in parentheses mean:

1. The note is being sustained over a system (note in standard notation is tied), or

2. The note is sustained, but a new articulation (such as a hammer-on, pull-off, slide, or vibrato begins), or

3. The note is a barely audible "ghost" note (note in standard notation is also in parentheses).

ADDITIONAL MUSICAL DEFINITIONS

 (accent) • Accentuate note (play it louder)

 (staccato) • Play the note short

D.S. al Coda • Go back to the sign (%), then play until the measure marked "*To Coda*," then skip to the section labelled "**Coda**."

D.C. al Fine • Go back to the beginning of the song and play until the measure marked "*Fine*" (end).

N.C. • No chord

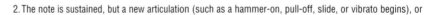

 • Repeat measures between signs.

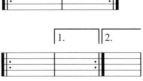
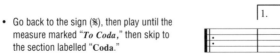 • When a repeated section has different endings, play the first ending only the first time and the second ending only the second time.

TRACK LIST/SONG INDEX

ABOUT THE AUTHORS

FRED SOKOLOW is a versatile "musician's musician." Besides fronting his own jazz, bluegrass, and rock bands, Fred has toured with Bobbie Gentry, Jim Stafford, Tom Paxton, Ian Whitcomb, Jody Stecher and The Limeliters, playing guitar, banjo, mandolin, and Dobro. His music has been heard on many TV shows (*Survivor, Dr. Quinn*), commercials, and movies (listen for his Dixieland-style banjo in *The Cat's Meow*).

Sokolow has written nearly a hundred stringed instrument books and videos for seven major publishers. This library of instructional material, which teaches jazz, rock, bluegrass, country, and blues guitar, banjo, Dobro, and mandolin, is sold on six continents. He also teaches musical seminars on the West Coast. A jazz CD, two rock guitar and two banjo recordings, which showcase Sokolow's technique, all received excellent reviews in the U.S. and Europe.

If you think Sokolow still isn't versatile enough, know that he emceed for Carol Doda at San Francisco's legendary Condor Club, accompanied a Russian balalaika virtuoso at the swank Bonaventure Hotel in L.A., won the *Gong Show*, played lap steel and banjo on the *Tonight Show*, picked Dobro with Chubby Checker, and played mandolin with Rick James. You can reach Fred and see his catalog of instructional material at **www.sokolowmusic.com**.

JIM BELOFF is the author of *The Ukulele—A Visual History* (Backbeat Books) and author, compiler, and/or publisher of the popular Jumpin' Jim's series of ukulele songbooks. This series has sold over 200,000 copies worldwide and is distributed by the Hal Leonard Corporation.

Jim has also recorded two CDs of original songs performed on the ukulele (*Jim's Dog Has Fleas* and *For the Love of Uke*), produced *Legends of Ukulele*, a CD compilation for Rhino Records, and made two how-to-play videos for Homespun Tapes entitled *The Joy of Uke #1* and *#2*. In 2004, he released *The Finer Things*, a recording of sixteen songs he co-wrote with ukulele master Herb Ohta.

In 1999, Jim and his family introduced a new, colorful, and low-cost ukulele called the FLUKE that has won admirers all over the world. In six years over 20,000 FLUKE and FLEA (a soprano-sized sibling of the FLUKE) ukuleles have been sold. In November 1999 he premiered his *Uke Can't Be Serious* concerto for ukulele and symphony orchestra. It was commissioned and performed with the Wallingford (Connecticut) Symphony. In 2002, Jim and his wife, Liz, were lead consultants on Ukulele Fever at the Stamford (CT) Museum. This exhibit was the first museum show to explore the full history of the ukulele. Their Los Angeles-based company, Flea Market Music, is dedicated to the ukulele and they believe very strongly that "Uke Can Change the World." You can reach Jim through the Flea Market Music website at **www.fleamarketmusic.com**.